CW00523740

CYCLE UK!
The essential guide
to leisure cycling

Les Lumsdon

Published by Sigma Leisure – an imprint of
Sigma Press, 1 South Oak Lane, Wilmslow, Cheshire SK9 6AR, England.

British Library Cataloguing in Publication Data
A CIP record for this book is available from the British Library.

ISBN: 1-85058-386-2

Typesetting and Design by: Sigma Press, Wilmslow, Cheshire.

Cover picture: Cycling near Church Stretton, Shropshire
(Chris Rushton).

Printed by: MFP Design & Print

Preface

It has taken a long time to come, but cycling for leisure is back again in a big way. The idea of going for a ride at the weekend is no longer a marginal activity, it is fast becoming an institution. Given the rapid rise of cycling, it is interesting to reflect on developments just a hundred years ago. The parallels are uncanny. The experimentation in manufacture of all types of cycles, for example, which occurred in the latter decades of the 19th century is happening again with new lighter models of unicycles, tricycles, 'sociables' and tandems in production. Also, the emergence of the safety bicycle and its variants, has been succeeded by the all terrain bike, and my guess is that the ATB will still be around in 2030.

In social terms, the renaissance of cycling is following a similar pattern. Historians will dismiss these views, no doubt, as too simplistic but the pattern of the take-up of leisure cycling is all-too familiar. The widening of interest from a narrow group to a mass market within ten years has been impressive in both Europe and the United States. The difference is that it is now happening in a society where the car dominates.

Mirroring this growth is the arrival of new cycling guides which outline scenic rides for the would-be rider. The early guides set out magnificent rides from railway networks, elaborately illustrated and written with abounding enthusiasm. More recent guides have tended to concentrate on off-road cycling, but Sigma Leisure (publishers of this book) have introduced a series of guides for the casual cycle tourer who is looking for 'away from it all' routes.

An important criterion for the casual cyclist is the need to find traffic-free links between town and country so that we can cycle from our homes in safety rather than battling with off-putting traffic for the first few miles. This is why this guide has been written: to help you find safe and enjoyable routes away from the bustle.

It is gratifying to note that many local authorities are looking seriously at providing more cycle paths, lanes and routes which are relatively traffic-free. I also recognise the exceptional work of organisations such as the Cyclists' Touring Club, Friends of the Earth and Transport 2000 in campaigning for the cyclist. My thanks go to them and all others who have supplied information for this book. Special thanks go to Pat Lumsdon for researching revisions for this edition.

Above all else my thanks go to Sustrans, cycle path designers and builders, an organisation which has championed the idea of linking town and countryside by using off-road routes for over a decade. For every copy of *Cycle UK!* sold, a small donation will be made to Sustrans (a registered charity) knowing that every mile of cycle path it manages to build means more hours of safe and enjoyable riding for the rest of us. *That's what cycling is all about!*

Les Lumsdon

Welcome to
CYCLE UK!

The United Kingdom has so much to offer cyclists. Away from the main cities and major highways, there are hundreds of kilometres of back roads which lead to a quieter Britain. It is here that you will find castles and churches, country inns and pretty cottages. There's also a great interest in off-road cycling and many forest and mountain paths are open to mountain bikers. This guide is a must if you want to go cycling for a weekend or to plan a longer tour.

Welcome to the United Kingdom and enjoy your cycling!

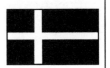

Willkommen zu *CYCLE UK!*

Großbritannien hat Rodfahrern so viel zu bieten. Abseits der Großstädte und Autobahnen kann man auf Hunderten von Kilometern über Nebenstraßen den Weg zu einem ruhigeren Großbritannien finden.

Gerade hier finden Sie Burgen und Kirchen, ländliche Gasthöfe und reizvolle Cottages. Den zahlreichen Mountainbikern, die sich für ``off-road cycling'' interessieren, sind viele Wälder und Gebirgs zugänglich. Dieser Reiseführer ist ein Muß für all jene die mit ihren Fahrrädern entweder nur einen Wochenendausflug machen wollen oder auch eine längere Tour planen.

Willkommen in Großbritannien und viel Spaß beim Radfahren!

Bienvenu au *CYCLE UK!*

Le Royaume-Uni a tant à offrir aux cyclistes. Eloignés des grandes villes et des grandes routes principales, il y a des centaines de kilomètres de petites routes qui mènent à une Grande-Bretagne plus calme.

C'est ici que vous trouverez châteaux et églises, auberges de campagne et ravissants cottages. Il y a également un grand intérêt à faire du vélo sur les petites routes, et de nombreux sentiers forestiers et montagnards sont ouverts aux vélos tout terrain. Ce Guide est un plus si vous voulez faire du vélo pour un week-end ou organiser un plus long voyage.

Bienvenus au Royaume-Uni et apprèçiez votre ballade cycliste!

Benvenuti a *CYCLE UK!*

Il Regno Unito ha tantissimo per offrire al ciclismo lontano dalle grande città e autostrade, ci sono centinaia di kilometri di piccole strade che conducono all' Inghilterra piu tranquilla.

È lì, dove si trovano dei castelli e chiese, alberghi e case di campagnia. È un luogo molto interessante per il ciclismo, che permettono ai ciclisti di esplorare, i cammini aperti nei boschi. Questa guida e indispensabile per organizzare delle vacanze in bicicletta per la fine settimana, o per vacanze piu lunghe.

Benvenuti all' Inghilterra vi auguriamo delle belle vacanze in bicicletta.

Bienvenidos a *CYCLE UK!*

El Reino Unido tiene tanto para ofrecer a ciclistas. Lejos de las grandes cuidades y autopistas, hay cientos de kilómetros de pequeñas calles que conducen a una más tranquila Inglaterra.

Es allí donde encontrarán castillos e iglesias, hoteles campestres y hermosas casas de campo, y un gran interés en ciclismo, con bosques y caminos abiertos a ciclistas. Esta guía es indispensable para organizar toures en bicicleta para los fines de semana o para planear viajes de mayor duración.

Bienvenidos al Reino Unido y que disfruten sus viajes en bicicleta!

"CYCLE UK" heet U van harte welkom!

Voor fietsers heeft Groot-Brittannië veel aan te bieden. Wag van de grote steden en drukke wegen, kunt U honderden kilometers van rustige straatjes en lanen vinden, die U naar het oorspronkelijke Engeland voeren met z'n oude kastelen en kerken, pittoreske ``cottage'' huisjes en, niet te vergeten, zijn beroemde ``country inn'' cafés.

Ook staan er veel bergweggetjes en bospaden ter beschikking voor de enthousiaste mountain bike fietser.

Kortom, voor een lange of korte fietstocht door Groot-Brittannië is deze gids precies wat U nodig hebt!

Wij wensen U veel plezier op de fiets in Groot-Britannië.

Velkom til *CYCLE UK!*

Storbritannien har virkelig meget at byde cykelister. Væk fra storbyerne og motorvejene, ligger hundredevis af kilometer mindre veje, som viser vej til et mere stille og roligt Storbritannien.

Det er her du kan finde mange slotte, borge, kirker, landsbykroer og yndige små huse. Der er også en stor interesse for off-road cykling, og mange skov – og bjergstier er åbne til mountainbikers.

Denne guide er nødvendig, hvis du ønsker dig en cykel-weekend eller planlægger en længere tur.

Velkom til Storbrittanien og god fornøjelse!

Contents

The Pleasures of Cycling

Regional Routes and Information

CYCLIST'S NOTEBOOK

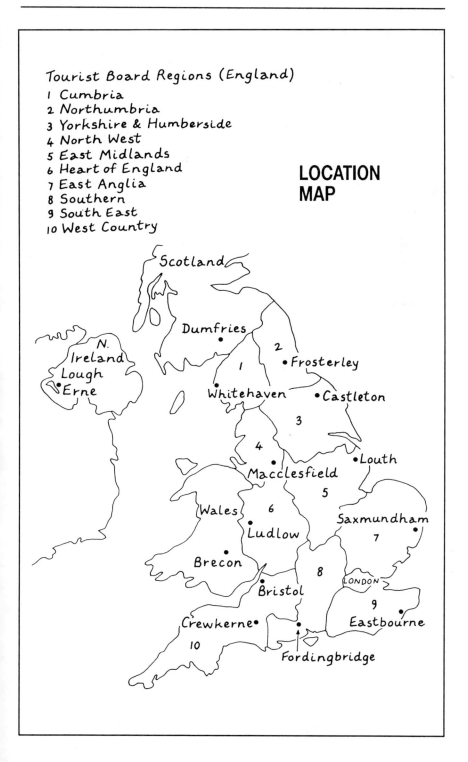

Tourist Board Regions (England)
1 Cumbria
2 Northumbria
3 Yorkshire & Humberside
4 North West
5 East Midlands
6 Heart of England
7 East Anglia
8 Southern
9 South East
10 West Country

LOCATION MAP

Scotland

Dumfries

N. Ireland
Lough Erne

2
Frosterley

1

Whitehaven • Castleton

3

4
Macclesfield

Louth

5

Wales

6

Ludlow

Saxmundham
7

Brecon

8

LONDON

Bristol

9

Crewkerne• Eastbourne

10

Fordingbridge

Opposite: a quiet corner in Montgomeryshire (Chris Rushton)

THE PLEASURES OF CYCLING

Cycling is Here to Stay!

Throughout the land you will find peaceful country lanes which bring village and town together, old by-ways which have been unsung through the ages as they lead to nowhere in particular. These are the lanes to be found in Western Herefordshire between Black and White villages and into Wales. These are the lanes alongside the water meadows of the Somerset Levels, the quiet climbs through the still, clean, cool air of the Scottish Borders. They make up a paradise that is largely undiscovered: a paradise of farm, hamlet, village pub and green, where the parish church has stood steadfast on higher ground through the ages. It is here that the cyclist begins to touch both the people and the landscape; where agriculture still dominates the way of life. These are the haunts of cyclists in earlier times and the ones we recreate for today. For the trends are with us. By every measure - cycle sales, hire, and holidays - cycling is here to stay!

Inspiration of The Past

These enchanting rural routes bring the cycle tourer to a countryside where reminders of past ages inspire more than a gaze: romantic abbey ruins, historic battlegrounds, or serene stately homes, all of which have a story to tell. They also bring you closer to wildlife, rabbits hopping across the road, a heron on the wing from nearby water, and the fox slyly making an exit along a hedge.

Freedom

But there are also off-road routes across windswept moorland, high level ground where ancient Iron and Bronze Age tribes once lived. Forest tracks augur well for the off-road rider too. They rise to summits with a vista between lines of conifers, suddenly plunging down to ford babbling streams, through bracken clad slopes or medieval pockets of woodland rich in insect and bird life. This is the new ground for the rider who is seeking freedom and a challenge.

Traffic-Free Routes

CYCLE UK! puts you in touch with this cycling paradise. It is packed with ideas for cycling which avoid the hassle of traffic, whether along specially devised cycle routes, stunning off-road mountain trails or genteel saunters through picturesque villages. It also puts you in touch with people in the cycle holiday and hire business throughout the UK who know their patch well and can advise you on the best local cycle rides. Riding in safety along traffic-free or lightly trafficked routes is, after all, one of the most accessible and refreshing experiences remaining in the late 20th century. The National Cycle Route will bring an extra dimension to this freedom.

The book refers to all quarters of the kingdom - England, Scotland, Wales and Northern Ireland. Wherever you travel there are places listed, contacts to make and cycling friends to gain. *CYCLE UK!* also refers to the Channel Islands and the Isle of Man (which, strictly speaking, are not in the UK). These islands offer very pleasant cycling so if you like the idea of an island hop pick up a 'phone to one of the cycling companies there and take a trip across the water.

20 MILLION CYCLISTS

There are an estimated 20 million owners of cycles in Britain. We use our cycles for all purposes, making more trips per year than users of the train and London Underground combined.

About a third of all of cycle journeys are estimated to be for leisure and this is likely to grow. There are more people than ever buying a bike for countryside rides!

Appeal of the Landscape

The changing nature of the UK landscape has the greatest appeal to the cyclist. Often within a few miles, or certainly a half-day ride, it is possible to witness coastline, valley and hill terrain. Millions of years of geological upheaval, from the laying of the oldest igneous rocks to the glacial sweeps of the Ice Ages, has formed this treasured landscape, one which has literally weathered through time. It is both wild and rugged, where impressive mountains tumble into lochs, craggy edges give way to deep ravines, and human endeavour is pitted against the elements. It is also gentle, a landscape where wolds unfold gently to green riverside pastures. There's no space here to discuss the detail of geology but roughly speaking there is a great divide in the land. Take a line from the River Tees in the North East to the Exe in the South West and the land to

3

the east forms gentler lowland Britain whereas to the west of this imaginary line is upland Britain, characterised by high hills and mountains. This is one of those generalisations which provides a useful yardstick when planning a tour. You can, as you know, find hills everywhere even when you are not looking for them!

Human Hand

It is the hand of humans, however, which makes the UK countryside so varied, a countryside husbanded by farming families from medieval times. The ravages of earlier times are still evident: Saxon and Danish language mapped into village names, old Roman Roads and settlements evidenced throughout. The pattern of Saxon domination over Celtic tribes repeats itself throughout history, and the castles and walled towns reflect the brutal power-seeking exploits of the Norman war-lords. Despite the continued struggles for annexation and power especially in Ireland and Scotland as well the bloody strife of the English Civil War life between wars settled much as beforehand to peaceful farming.

Changing Patterns

During the past 250 hundred years the encroaching process of industrialisation has changed the landscape. The building of textile mills by fast-flowing streams, and the coming of canals and railways must have been a traumatic experience for a rural people, as this ruined some of their finest scenery. Small market towns either took on a regained economic significance or withered alongside the old coaching routes. Given these momentous changes and a relentless migration of country folk to the squalor of burgeoning Victorian towns it seems hard to digest the argument that the greatest changes to the countryside are occurring now.

The major changes are of an agrarian nature particularly the intense mechanisation of farming, the enlargement of fields requiring the grubbing of hedges, and the extensive use of chemicals to increase yields. The threats are many-fold, but most observers are concerned that the rich wildlife and flora of certain landscapes will be lost forever. We have great expectations of our farmers and of those who seek to conserve the countryside for future generations. The hope is that the balance will revert to conservation without unduly impairing economic gain.

Calming Traffic

There's another threat. Those of us living in towns now visit the countryside more often and demand more of it. In particular, the use of the car in the countryside is becoming increasingly threatening. The car is not only bringing congestion to honey-pot areas but also endangers other road users such as walkers, horse riders and cyclists. Some are driving faster than is responsible along roads which were made for the horse and cart rather than a high-powered vehicle. Taming the car in the countryside, known technically as "traffic calming", can only come about if we seek to enjoy the countryside's splendour by using other forms of transport. Your support to keep our "green and pleasant land" is enlisted through these pages.

HATS ON!

The debate about whether cycling helmets do or do not provide safer cycling will continue to rage throughout the 1990s but one thing is for sure – if a helmet avoids even a slight injury it is worth wearing one.

Helmets offer no protection against cars going at greater speeds than is sensible. The only way to ride is confidently but defensively where traffic is a threat. Do not assume that car drivers will give way to you nor give you sufficient space to ride in safety when they overtake. Be seen too! Wear bright clothing and always have your lights on when the weather is poor and after dark.

Cycling Provision is on the Increase

Fortunately, the provision of routes suitable for cyclists is increasing at a great pace, not great enough some would argue, but certainly rapid in comparison to five years ago. There are hundreds of suggestions for day and weekend rides where the paradise talked about earlier still exists, i.e. car free and lightly trafficked areas. Go for them. Enjoy a healthy, pollution-free break which, to coin a phrase, "does not cost the earth". It is a sentiment which is being echoed throughout the land.

A WELCOME TO OVERSEAS VISITORS

It goes without saying that overseas visitors are welcome to the UK! Your holiday here can be so much better if you escape the busy tourist haunts which are often not cycle friendly and are geared mainly to looking after large numbers of visitors. By detouring a little you come across different landscapes and regional variations in culture and cuisine. The pace is not so hectic either and you can return home having enjoyed a little of Britain which most overseas visitors do not encounter.

There are a few key points which you need to remember before you travel:

❏ By law you have to cycle on the left side of the road (rather than the right). Practise left and right turns before venturing onto a road! The right turn is especially important as this proves to be a risky manoeuvre for all cyclists here.

❏ While the kilometre, as a measurement of distance, is becoming more familiar, most people in the UK still use "miles" (1 mile = 1.6 km). Signposts illustrate distances in "miles" and most leaflets and guidebooks give distances in miles. One mile is 1600 metres.

❏ Cyclists are not allowed to cycle on pavements or in pedestrian areas unless special paths are provided or a sign indicates the contrary.

❏ Cyclists are allowed on most roads except motorways (which would be suicidal anyway) but avoid "A" roads as they tend to be very busy and attract heavy lorries.

❏ It is possible to use bridleways, by-ways, and tracks where cycling is allowed by the landowner but it is sometimes difficult to know which ones are available. Bridleways are shown by a horse on a wooden or metal sign. It is also possible to use canal towpaths sometimes. See *Cyclists Notebook*).

❏ If bringing your own bike make sure that you have spares if it is an older or specialist model. There is usually a cycle shop in most towns, however, which will have spares which might fit your bike. Spare parts for new bicycles are more likely to be standard between countries and there should be no problem getting a suitable replacement here.

❏ Refreshment is not always available when you want it. There are usually plenty of pubs, but fewer cafés. Pubs can sometimes be closed at lunchtimes in rural areas during the winter but otherwise you'll find that most open between noon and three and in the evening from 6pm (7pm on Sundays) again until 11pm (10.30pm on Sundays). Some pubs in towns (including small ones) stay open all day and so do some country pubs on Saturdays. Food, however, is usually available between noon and 2pm and from early evening until 9.30pm. If you find this frustrating, so do many British people. But it is improving!

HOW TO USE THIS BOOK

CYCLE UK! is divided into Tourist Board Regions running from the South West of England to Scotland, then Wales, Northern Ireland, the Channel Islands and Isle of Man. Each region is covered in separate sections, as follows:

▼ **Introduction:**
> A general note about what the region has to offer.

▼ **A One-Day or Two-Day Country Ride:**
> These have been contributed with great enthusiasm by cycle companies, tourism officers or the author. They include both off-road and road routes of varying degrees of difficulty:

Region	Location	Mileage	Grade	Bike
West Country	Bristol and Bath	40	Easy	T
West Country	South Somerset	61	Easy	T
Southern	New Forest	34	Easy	T
South East	South Downs	14	Mod	ATB
Heart of England	Shropshire	46	Mod	T
East Anglia	East Suffolk	60	Easy	T
East Midlands	Lincolnshire Wolds	80	Easy	T
North West	Western Peakland & Staffordshire Moors	32	Mod/ Hard	T
Humberside & Yorkshire	North York Moors	36	Mod/ Hard	ATB
Cumbria	Western Cumbria	64	Mod/ Hard	T
Northumbria	Weardale	40	Hard	T
Scotland	Dumfries	60	Mod	T
Wales	Brecon Beacons	30	Hard	ATB
Northern Ireland	Lough Erne	52	Easy/ Mod	T

Notes:

T - Any bicycle suitable for touring; ATB - All Terrain Bike able to withstand a rougher ride; (On the Cumbria ride there are one or two suggested diversions for those with ATBs)

Grading: Based mainly on climbs involved: 'Easy' refers to routes where there are a limited number of climbs and where none are ferocious; 'Moderate' suggests that more stamina is required, for there will be steeper hills and more of them; 'Hard' refers to a greater number of climbs often on steep tracks and where the descents are also steep therefore requiring greater skill and care.

'Great Cycling Ideas'

In these sections you will find lists of routes and ways which have been publicised in recent years for use by cyclists. They are mainly off-road, and some are shared with other users such as horse riders. Others refer to road tours which use quiet unclassified roads where traffic levels are low. Some are waymarked, others are not. Most are publicised by a leaflet or booklet. Very few of these publications are free but most cost very little and are generally available from local tourist information centres. They are invaluable for the recreational cyclist and you will find them listed in alphabetical order by county (although counties may change size and shape, even their names, during the lifetime of this book).

Cycling at Wetton Mill, Staffordshire Moorlands (Chris Rushton)

Cycle Holiday & Hire Companies

▼ Cycle Holidays

These are listed in alphabetical order in each region. They offer first-class holidays ranging from short breaks to full touring holidays. Most are self-guided but some are led by a guide and, in some cases, baggage handling is offered between accommodation stops, which is a very civilised touch.

Several companies offer specialised mountain bike breaks and training. You will see that several offer cycle hire, too.

▼ Cycle Hire

Known cycle hire companies are listed on a county basis in each region. They are listed by location. Therefore, if you are staying in Cornwall and want to cycle from Newquay local hire will be listed under that place name.

CYCLING ABROAD

The world is a big place but there are cycle tours to all four corners. First call should be to the CTC who offer an extensive range of tours, as do Bike Tours in Bath. Specialist tour companies offer a range of tours from Africa to Latin America.

Most people initially settle for Europe and leaders in the field are:

Anglo Dutch Sport, 30a Foxgrove Rd, Beckenham, Kent BR3 2BD.
Tel: 0181 650 2347.

Bents Bicycle Tours, The Priory, High St, Redbourn, Hertfordshire, AL3 7LZ.
Tel: (01582) 793249

Cycling For Softies, 2-4 Birch Polygon, Manchester M14 5HX. Tel: 0161 248 8282

Fresco Cycling Holidays, Alternative Travel Group, 69-71 Banbury Road, Oxford, OX2 6PE. Tel: (01865) 310244

HeadWater Holidays, Northwich, Cheshire CW9 5BR. Tel: (01606) 48699

There are several other good tour companies who advertise in the key magazines.

PLANNING A DAY OUT

✔ If you have your own bike, check it is in good shape mechanically.

✔ Seek from Tourist Information any leaflets and guides for the destinations listed under 'Cycling Ideas' and off you go!

✔ Remember to pack your *Action Kit* (see below).

✔ Check Cycle Hire facilities.

Those interested in cycle hire should read the next few paragraphs:

The people who run cycle hire and holidays tend to be good sorts. They are mostly cyclists themselves who like to share their knowledge and interest with the rest of us. They know the patch, often the pubs and places of interest. They also well understand the joys of a good day's ride and the disappointment that comes when there is a hitch. They virtually all stock ATBs or Mountain Bikes. Some will also have touring bikes, recumbents, tandems, unicycles and wheelchair bikes. Most cater for children and a small number have trailers for use.

A wheelchair tandem on the Tarka Trail in Devon, on hire from Bideford Bicycle Hire (Vivien M. Tregellas)

Many cycle-hire locations in towns tend to be long-standing cycle traders who offer hire alongside cycle sales and repair. They do it to provide a full service to customers and maybe you'll even consider buying a bike to take home! Often, they have only a few bikes on offer - particularly during the winter months as most of the hire bikes are sold off before Christmas. All traders will ask for a guarantee before you hire - i.e. a cheque or a credit card slip made out for an agreed sum. You are expected to take good care of the bike, i.e. no skidding stunts, wheelies, or kerb smashing stuff as this can damage the bike and you! Many a cycle trader has stopped hiring for this very reason.

As with all businesses, some hirers are better than others when looking after you. You feel more assured if the company makes sure that you and the bike fit, by checking your size and the frame of the bike before marrying the two of you together.

It is also useful if gears and brakes are explained as they might differ from your own bike or when you last cycled. They should also provide you with a "back up" kit if things go wrong. This only takes a few minutes at the time of hire.

The Cycle Hirer's checklist (see *Cyclist's Notebook* at the back of this book) is worth more than a glance.

MAINTAIN YOUR BIKE!

A little maintenance goes a long way! Basic maintenance is not a long task and there are several books on the market which explain how to do easy tasks (such as *Richard's New Bicycle Book*) and there are weekend courses to learn such skills.

The main checks you should make before cycling are:

Brakes – Check that the brake blocks are adjusted to fit the rim (approximately one millimetre from it and lined up). Run your fingers along the cable to the handlebars to ensure that there are no worn sections.

Chain – Ensure that it is not slack and is sufficiently lubricated.

Gears – Minor adjustments can be made to the gear changing parts but if there is a problem it might be best to check with your dealer.

Tyres – Ensure that the tread is not worn and that the valves are intact. Pump up tyres regularly but not too hard.

Wheels – Look for broken or bent spokes and buckled wheels. If damaged, the bike will have to go in to the shop a check up.

Lights – Must be in working order and a bell or horn fitted.

If you do not feel confident about fixing you own bike simply take it into your local cycle dealer. Most offer a repair and maintenance service.

Entries in CYCLE UK!

The list in this book covers most of the UK, the Channel Islands and the Isle of Man, but it is not definitive. There are cycle hire locations not mentioned here. What you find in these pages are the hirers who have taken the time to respond positively to a brief questionnaire sent out to them. These are centres that are committed to providing you with a good service.

It is sad but, during the lifetime of the book, several will go out of business for a variety of reasons. There are others who have not responded to my call for action or have started up since then. Your feedback about those included here or new discoveries will be most welcome. Simply send in the comments form at the back of the book if you find the details to be incorrect or not current. The aim is to make *CYCLE UK!* bigger and better as the years go by.

> ### Cycle Hire and
> ### Holiday Information in
> ### *CYCLE UK!*
> **Availability:** the months shown are inclusive. Some cycle hire locations are not open on Sundays (e.g. bicycle shops in towns) so check before travelling.
>
> **BR:** denotes where a cycle hire centre is in a town or village served by railway

PLANNING A TOUR

Cycling Holidays

Choosing a company for a short break, an activity holiday or a longer touring holiday requires a little more thinking-through than a casual day hire. Pick up the 'phone and you tend to get the measure of the company fairly quickly. Brochure material also provides an indication of how a company presents itself. Most of the companies listed in these pages have been in business for several years and understand customer needs well. Nevertheless, it is worth looking over the *Holiday Checklist* before you speak to them or make a booking (see *Cyclist's Notebook*).

YOUR ACTION KIT

Whether you are out on your own bike or a hired cycle, check that you have these essentials with you. A puncture is annoying, but as long as you know the rudiments of repair (often to be found on the repair kit) then it is an inconvenience of 15 minutes only. If anything serious goes wrong (and it rarely does on a day ride or short tour) it is best to call out the hire company or take your bike to a repair shop in a nearby town (hopefully there is a nearby town!).

> ### LOCK UP!
>
> Whenever you stop lock your bicycle up preferably to a solid object. The best place is where people are passing all of the time or where you can see it.
>
> Write yourself a card which includes the frame identity number and an accurate description of the bike. A photograph is even better. It can be used when advising the police about a theft if it occurs.

Here is the basic survival kit:

✔ Puncture Repair Outfit

✔ A pump

✔ A spare inner tube

✔ An all-purpose spanner and a tyre lever

✔ Lock or, even better, locks

✔ A note which describes the bicycle, make, registration number and any other relevant information in case it is stolen and you need to inform the police.

✔ Wipes to clean your hands

✔ Maps - Ordnance Survey Landrangers are fine for cycle touring

✔ Waterproofs

✔ A snack and drink

✔ Lights

✔ Insect repellent if it is a hot day

Mountain Biking

If fun and dirt (the no-smut variety) is what you are looking for, mountain biking has to be for you. It is exhilarating stuff and a hot bath at the end of the day is absolute bliss. With a little preparation you can find graded routes which suit your capabilities and within hours you can gain the basic skills of mountain biking, essential if you are not going to wreck the bike or more importantly yourself.

Despite the glamour image of mountain biking, it is not as easy as it looks. If you are really interested in taking mountain biking up seriously, sign up for a weekend with one of the companies specialising in mountain bike breaks and training courses. In this way you can learn the riding techniques first hand, get to grips with mountain bike codes and build confidence (and stamina) without bad biking habits.

One essential book for mountain bikers is the "Off-Road Cycling Trail Guide" which lists (and lists they are!) 700 off-road cycle opportunities. This neat little book summarises, for example, routes written up by other people, bridleways which exist on the ground as well as being shown on the map, and other matters, by county. It also gives addresses of the main providers of off-road cycling opportunities in England and Wales. The guide is written by Colin Palmer, an experienced off-road cyclist and is published by *Off-road Cycling*, Coddington, Ledbury, Hereford-shire HR8 1JH. Tel: (01531) 633500.

The controversy about mountain biking in the UK continues to rage, as elsewhere in the world. The main argument presented against the mountain biker is that too many riders arrive in groups to use too few tracks and bridleways which have for decades have been little used. The result has been some erosion of softer surfaces (nothing in comparison to what a tractor does to a track), a concern about disturbance to wildlife and an angry call from other users disturbed by groups of mountain bikers riding without care or courtesy. This had led to calls for a clamp-down on cycling off-road.

The truth of the matter is that there is a sustained and growing

---

SAFETY FIRST!

Make sure the bike is in good order

Tell a friend where you intend to cycle

Take small change for a phone box

Take a small first aid kit in a pannier

Wear clothing that can be seen and a helmet

Off-road cycling should be tackled gradually to build up skills demand for off-road cycling. After all, you don't have to climb up mountains to get fun out of ATBs. Cross country cycling is a great way to enjoy the countryside and does not require such pedal power as a mountainside. Both are great fun and a brilliant way to let off steam. No one wants to despoil sensitive countryside areas so, if you are taking up mountain biking, simply go for the areas where mountain bikers are welcomed.

The Forestry Commission, several progressive local authorities and a host of other organisations are now looking to cater increasingly for off-road cyclists. There are also dozens of local clubs so join one to find out how to improve your skills - contact the CTC, (see *Cyclist's Notebook*).

The reputation of mountain bikers has been badly bruised but, if you remember the code and head for the increasing number of routes being made available, then matters can only improve. The off-road cycling code is towards the end of this book.

Cyclists at Longborough in the Cotswolds (Gloucestershire County Council)

15

The Joy of Traffic-free Trails

The main problem for those people who have not cycled for a while, or families with young children, is traffic or - more to the point - how to avoid it. Your prayers are answered (partially at least) because Sustrans, the UK's major cycle-path designers, are in the process of building routes throughout the country which bridge town and countryside. They use mainly old railway tracks which are segregated from main roads. The Sustrans cycle-paths well illustrate what many people want. Over a million cyclists are estimated to use the Bristol to Bath path every year. We need more of these paths - and sooner rather than later.

CYCLING IS GOOD FOR YOU!

More than one survey has shown that cycling is good for you.

Cycling in a safe environment offers a good way to get healthy as it lowers the risk of heart attack, helps you to shed excess weight and reduces stress.

Seek out off-road paths or choose quieter roads to start your fitness campaign. If you don't believe it all obtain a copy of ``Cycling: Toward Health and Safety''. published by the British Medical Association. It contains the hard facts rather than the soft sell!

Philip Insall of Sustrans describes one such route in the "West Country" section. This is an ideal ride for those starting or coming back to cycling for leisure. There are dozens of similar routes throughout the country listed in this book.

Opposite: Cycling for all! (Dumfries and Galloway Tourist Board)

REGIONAL
ROUTES
& INFORMATION

THE WEST COUNTRY

This includes the counties of Avon, Cornwall, Devon, Dorset, Somerset, Wiltshire & The Isles of Scilly

Tourist Information: West Country Tourist Board, 60 St David's Hill, Exeter, EX4 4SY. Tel: (01392) 76351

Unusually, in this section there are two 'countryside rides' - this is because the Bristol to Devizes route is of historic importance, and also because the West Country is probably the most popular area for casual cycling in the UK.

One of England's favourite holiday destinations, the West Country has bustling seaside resorts such as Newquay, Torbay, Weymouth and Weston-super-Mare. It also has a variety of landscapes from the rugged sea cliffs of Land's End to the terraced hillsides of Wiltshire. Cornwall and Devon are a maze of narrow winding lanes where ancient hedgerows luxuriant in vegetation are to be found. Somerset is known for the tranquillity of the Levels and for the beauty of the Mendip hills, Cheddar Gorge and show caves. Avon, Dorset and Wiltshire are special to those who enjoy the miles of back lanes which lead to the historic settlements of Abbotsbury and Cerne Abbass, Avebury and Stonehenge, to thatched cottages and cream teas. There are, of course, the Isles of Scilly: of small dimensions and in many respects shy of tourists. A bike and boat expedition from Penzance might appeal to sea lovers.

There are two national parks in the West Country, Dartmoor and Exmoor, both exhibiting high moorland features and the former characterised by its weathered granite outcrops. It is not difficult to escape the crowds in these parks, especially if you are willing to climb the steep 'C-class' roads off the beaten track. Nevertheless, the main roads suffer unbearable traffic in the summer.

Joy for the cyclist in the West Country can be found in two ways: travelling on the excellent off-road cycling paths such as the Camel Trail in Cornwall, the Tarka Trail in Devon, the Avon and Wiltshire cycleways and the Bristol to Bath cycle path. Also, seek out the many quiet routes away from the seaside. Within a ten-minute ride from Penzance or St Ives there are back lanes which take you to the ruins of Iron Age Chyauster, or the ancient wayside village of Zennor. The same applies to the East Looe or Plym Valleys in Devon, the Blackdown or Quantock hills on the Somerset borders. They are all places of beauty where the cyclist can relax. The adventure of travelling by bike through Thomas Hardy's Wessex country or across the Wiltshire Downs brings equal reward.

COUNTRYSIDE RIDE

From Bristol to Devizes

Philip Insall of Sustrans

Distance: 40 miles.

Terrain: mainly off-road and easy going; suitable for all cyclists.

Maps: O.S. Landranger 172 Bristol, Bath and surrounding area and 173, Swindon, Devizes and surrounding area.

Rail Access: Bristol Temple Meads, Bath, Freshford, Avoncliffe, Bradford-on-Avon.

Accommodation and Refreshment: There are inns and canal-side tea gardens interspersed along the route and ample bed and breakfast throughout. Main Tourist Information centres are: Bristol - (0117) 926 0767; Bath - (01225) 462831; Bradford-on-Avon - (01225) 865797; Devizes - (01380) 729408.

Cycle Hire: There is cycle hire available at Bristol, Bath and Bradford-on-Avon. Check the *CYCLE UK!* entry under Avon and Wiltshire in the West Country section.

Cycling on The Kennet & Avon Canal Towpath: Please check details regarding permission to use the towpath before cycling on this route. See `Cycling on Waterways' in the Cyclist's *Notebook* at the end of this book.

The Ride

The ride follows the Bristol and Bath Railway path between these historic cities and then runs along the towpath of the Kennet and Avon canal to Devizes. It is a linear route which can be accessed at Bristol, Bath or Devizes as well as in the many villages on the route. Ride part of it as a day outing or alternatively, choose overnight accommodation *en route* before returning to your starting point.

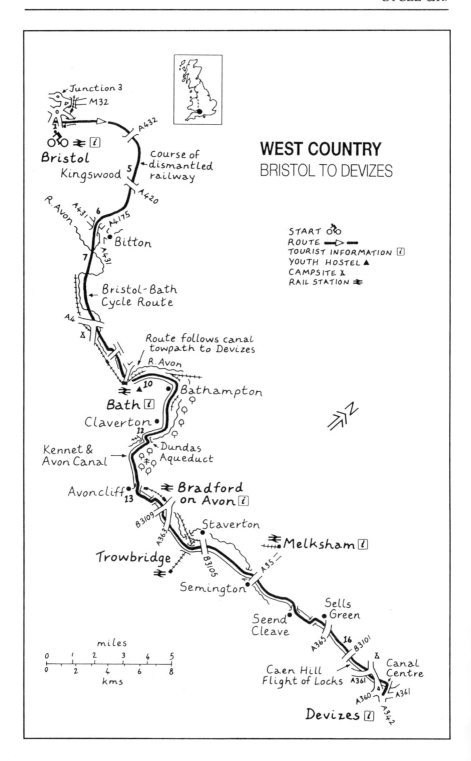

WEST COUNTRY
BRISTOL TO DEVIZES

START
ROUTE
TOURIST INFORMATION
YOUTH HOSTEL
CAMPSITE
RAIL STATION

Junction 3
M32
Bristol
Kingswood

Course of
dismantled
railway

A432

R. Avon
A431
A4175
Bitton
A431

Bristol-Bath
Cycle Route

A4

Route follows canal
towpath to Devizes
R. Avon

Bathampton
Bath
Claverton

Kennet &
Avon Canal

Dundas
Aqueduct

Avoncliff
Bradford
on Avon

Staverton

Melksham
Trowbridge
B3105
A35
Semington

Seend
Cleave

Sells
Green

A365
B3101
Canal
Centre
Caen Hill
Flight of Locks
A361
A360
A361
A342
Devizes

miles
0   1   2   3   4   5
0   2   4   6   8
kms

Seeing Places

Bristol: Bristol grew up as a major trading centre throughout the ages despatching ships to the four corners of the world. It no longer functions as a commercial port but the harbour and waterfront reflect its rich maritime heritage including the magnificent *SS Great Britain* designed by Isambard Kingdom Brunel. At the wharf in Redcliff Way you can see the reconstruction of Matthew, the ship in which John Cabot discovered Newfoundland. In 1997 the ship will recreate the historic voyage.

Bath: made famous by the rich of the 17th century, Bath enjoys a wealth of elegant Georgian architecture which visitors come in their thousands to see. The central area is ideal for walking for traffic has been kept out. A visit to the abbey, pump rooms and Roman Baths makes locking up your bike worthwhile.

Bradford-on-Avon: this historic hillside town of mellow stone grew up with the wool trade. It has several attractions and a good centre for browsing in shop windows.

Devizes: a town which grew up around its castle, Devizes was built in the 11th century and suffered much damage during the English Civil War. This characterful old Georgian centre is well-known to real ale fans as the home of Wadworth brewery.

Kennet and Avon Canal: in the second decade of the 19th century, the Kennet and Avon Canal Company was born to bridge the gap between the river Kennet and River Avon - hence the name of the navigation. The company succeeded in the early years but, as with so many canals, trade declined with the coming of the railways. In the 1950s the canal fell into disrepair but through the stalwart work of the Kennet and Avon Canal Trust in association with British Waterways and other bodies the canal has been restored throughout the past thirty years. For more details 'phone (01380) 721279. Please check with British Waterways locally before cycling on the towpath (see *Cyclist's Notebook*).

The Route

1. The Bristol and Bath Railway path begins in an inauspicious-looking light industrial estate on St Philip's Road, off Midland Road, close to the centre of Bristol. Where St Philip's Road turns left to join Trinity Street, go straight on under a huge wooden gateway celebrating the

completion of the path by Cyclebag (the pressure group which grew to become Sustrans) in 1984.

2. The path ducks and dives a little, past large garishly painted tower blocks and underneath the obligatory new urban motorway. There are several other access points into the Railway Path around Barrow Road, Lawrence Hill and through Easton. At Brixton Road, you find the first sculpture: a drinking fountain - Steve Joyce's "Dancing Drum". Travel along to Clay Bottom where there is a fine vista over the city of Bristol and the Clay Bottom viaduct.

The Dancing Drum (Sustrans)

3. Pass by the Elizabeth Shaw chocolate factory, marked by a succulent aroma of confectionery and then by a supermarket where a giant brick fish can be seen diving into a brick pond. The district is known as Fishponds, you see. Through the Staple Hill Tunnel and look out for a mosaic high up on the left as you leave.

4. You arrive at Mangotsfield old railway station. This was to be demolished by the local council but Sustrans has restored the building and made a sculpture garden there instead. This is also the junction for a cycle route to Yate. Your way is ahead, however, through Rodway Hill and Siston Common but the way is to be

re-routed from the disused railway track bed to accommodate an urban fringe road of motorway proportions.

5. Go through Warmley old station with its handsome signal box, bike repair workshop, and amazing sculpture then cross the main A420 road. Next stop is Gaius Sentius, an enormous reclining Roman who looks as though it's something other than water he's been drinking. That's what flows into his mouth, though, when you press the button.

6. Shortly after crossing Southway Drive, you'll come alongside railway tracks. The Bitton Railway Society has a marvellous selection of old rolling stock: most of it works, and at any time you may see a steam train chuntering purposefully alongside the path. The Society is now extending their tracks south of Bitton - interesting proof that the railway can co-exist well with cyclists and walkers. Incidentally, the station café is very friendly with good cakes and coffee too!

7. You now come to two railway bridges over the River Avon. Look for the Saxon relics and the seat carved by Jim Partridge and Liz Walmsley from a wind-blown oak. You will also see Dominic Lowery's four carved mileposts. Ideally placed here is the Bird in Hand pub for those in need of refreshment. One more river bridge and you reach Brassmill Lane. This is the end of the Railway Path and the start of the riverside path.

8. Riverside paths always have pubs and the Dolphin pub to be found along this section is worth a stop. Come up the ramp onto Churchill Bridge. Go straight on across the road. This is the only tricky crossing on the whole route, so take care as you cross over. Continue straight along the pavement with the river to your right and cross to the right over the footbridge, a point which is only 50 metres from Bath Spa railway station and a possible cut off for those seeking an early return to Bristol (or it could be a starting point).

9. Under the railway bridge, with the river on your left, go along Claverton Street for a hundred metres or so: the pavement is wide enough for cautious riders and children to wheel a bike as this is a typical dual carriageway. At the Thimble Mill pub, an entry on the left of the road is signposted. Turn right onto the towpath and follow the Kennet and Avon canal for a couple of hundred metres, then up to and across the road. Now alongside the Widcombe flight of locks, with lots of ducks and greenery growing out of the lock gates, the view over Bath is superb.

10. Now carry your bike up a flight of steps to Bathwick Hill. Stores here sell all the ingredients of a picnic if you need one. Turn right

onto the road, and then left down a steep ramp on the other side of the bridge. Canals, like railway lines, run behind the facade of a city. Oddly, the backside of Bath is at least as beautiful as its façade, and this section of towpath is stunning. At Cleveland House the path climbs a steep ramp: don't go onto the road but turn left in front of the house. Cross the canal and go down a hairpin descent to the towpath now on the opposite bank and underneath the house!

11. Many people prefer to walk here, not only for reasons of caution but to admire the view. Please be considerate to walkers along the towpath and especially under bridges where the path narrows. Common sense and courtesy allow all users to enjoy this superb asset. Pass under a couple of lovely ironwork bridges, then another tunnel under the Warminster Road. Now the towpath emerges to an embankment above the railway, and the country views begin in earnest.

12. Cross the canal just before the Dundas Bridge. It would be easy to miss the sign here. When you see the turning pool before the aqueduct cross over the tiny stone bridge and continue round behind a small brick building. Go over a new steel lifting bridge (with a great sound when you go over it) and cross the aqueduct with the canal on your left. Look down at the view! At this point the canal runs along a wood, between hedges, lovely and secluded. Don't miss the Fordside tea gardens, through the hedge.

13. Next stop, the aqueduct at Avoncliffe. Pause to take in the view. After crossing, turn right and go down a steep road, under the aqueduct and then steeply up the other side turning sharp right and left back on to the canal bank. There's refreshment here too for those in need or a little farther along at Bradford Lock.

14. Take care here, where the towpath comes up to the road by a rather dangerous bridge over the canal. Turn right onto the road and then off to the left just before it crosses the canal. At the lock is the Kennet and Avon Canal Trust office, from which boat trips are available at certain times.

15. Just before Bradford Marina is the Beehive Inn, a possible overnight camping spot. Otherwise pass the Canal estate near Trowbridge (where there is a railway station). Now brace yourself for a shock as you approach the modern development at Hilperton. Close your eyes and pedal as fast as you can towards the flat meadows of Semington. The Somerset Arms is worth the detour, but beware of the signs on the road bridge which seem to suggest you should swim

the canal to get there! This section is well-known for good pubs nearby to the canal.

16. Continue ahead along the towpath to Lower Foxhangers Farm, crossing over the canal on a very old and pretty brick bridge and starting on the Caen Hill flight, the signature flight of locks that lead to Devizes. It is quite a haul up after a forty-mile trip. Take a look back at the view. If you are staying in Devizes overnight its worth walking back at sunset to look west over the locks and holding ponds towards Bristol and the Coast, and say to yourself... "I did it."

17. Return by the same route to Trowbridge, Bradford or Bath where a train space can be booked or return the entire route by cycle. You won't be disappointed for the vistas are as appealing from the canal in this direction. Whatever you decide, enjoy your night in Devizes. You've earned it.

This route is now part of the Sustrans' National Cycle Network. If you enjoy this trip you can look forward to much more safe cycling in the next century.

Cycling in South Somerset (Somerset Tourism)

COUNTRYSIDE RIDE

Across The Fosse Way in South Somerset

A two-day ride devised by
Jean Atkin and Sophy Cushing of Level Pedalling

Distance: 61 miles.

Terrain: easy going; suitable for all on-road bikes.

Maps: OS Landranger maps - 193 Taunton and Lyme Regis; and 182 Weston-super-Mare and Bridgwater.

Rail Access: Crewkerne where the ride begins.

Accommodation and Refreshment: Recommended accommodation is available from Level Pedalling or at the South Somerset Tourist Information. Tel: (01935) 71279. There are ample places to stop *en route* for refreshment.

Cycle Holidays and Guided Tours: Level Pedalling (01460) 72156.

The Ride

Quiet back lanes winding through the gently unfolding lands of South Somerset make this very pleasant cycling country. The mixture of grazing pastures, wetlands and cider orchards as you ride out from the historic centre of Crewkerne bring variety to the ride but the joy lies as much in the wealth of attractions within such reasonable pedalling distances.

The land flattens as you ride north from Crewkerne, and conversely becomes steeper as you return but climbs are invariably short. The route almost entirely follows quiet back lanes, but includes three short stretches of busier roads. It is recommended that you take two days but a cut-off has been suggested for those who have only a day to spare.

Seeing Places

Cider, willows and wetlands, pottery and divine gardens are all to be seen on this ride.

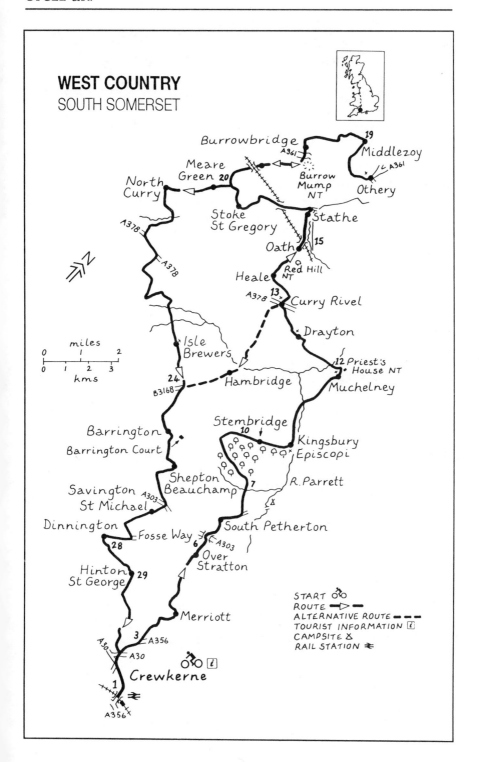

WEST COUNTRY
SOUTH SOMERSET

Burrowbridge
A361
19
Middlezoy

Meare
Green **20**
Burrow
Mump
NT
A361
Othery

North
Curry

Stoke
St Gregory
Stathe

A378

Oath
15

Heale
Red Hill
NT

A378 **13**
Curry Rivel

Drayton

miles
0   1   2
0   1   2   3
kms

Isle
Brewers

12 Priest's
House NT

24
B3168
Hambridge
Muchelney

Stembridge
10

Barrington
Barrington Court

Kingsbury
Episcopi

Shepton
Beauchamp
7
R. Parrett

Savington
St Michael
A303

Dinnington
Fosse Way
6 A303
South Petherton

28
Over
Stratton

Hinton
St George **29**

Merriott

3 A356

A30
A30

Crewkerne [i]

1

A356

START 🚲
ROUTE ▷—
ALTERNATIVE ROUTE ▬ ▬ ▬
TOURIST INFORMATION [i]
CAMPSITE ⊼
RAIL STATION ⇌

East Lambrook Manor Garden: Created by the late Margery Fish and made famous through her many books and lectures, this is both a traditional cottage style garden and an important collection of plants. The gardens extend around two sides of the rambling stone and brick house built in the 1470s, once thatched and now Somerset tiled. In 1938, when discovered by Margery Fish and her husband, it was derelict and rat infested; the garden was a wilderness. It is now attractive in all seasons.

Burrow Hill Cider Farm: Most of the vintage apples used for cider making are grown in the orchards at the farm, and are still pressed and fermented there. There is also a display of huge copper stills, and in the cider house, all of the paraphernalia associated with 150 years of cider-making. The cider can be sampled, as can the Somerset Royal Cider Brandy which is produced here too. Burrow Hill Cider is the first full cider distillery to be licensed in England, and the craft of distilling is being revived again in Somerset.

John Leach's Pottery, Mulcheney: John Leach, grandson of celebrated potter Bernard Leach, continues the family tradition from his own picturesque thatched workshops and shop just south of the ancient Somerset Levels village of Mulcheney. He has established an inter-national reputation for his hand-thrown Mulcheney kitchen pots based on the simple strength of English country pottery. The pots are fired in a traditional wood-fired kiln.

Mulcheney Abbey, Church and Priest's House: The abbey's remaining buildings are part of the abbot's lodgings, all that is left of the Benedic-tine monastery which was founded in 693 AD on what was then an island. The abbot's lodgings were rebuilt in Tudor Gothic style and stand as testimony to the grandeur of monastic life-style in the 15th and 16th centuries.

The parish church is early 15th century, built on earlier foundations. The wagon roof inside was transformed between 1600-25 by a local man who painted it with laughing, topless angels in Tudor costume, enjoying a heavenly life. There are also fragments of medieval tiles. The Priest's House stands opposite the church, a thatched 14th century house with a medieval two-storey hall and a 16th century Gothic window.

The Route

1. Turn right out of Crewkerne Station and wheel downhill into Crewkerne past a petrol station on the right. Continue along what is now a built-up street until you.pass Bicycle World cycle shop on your right and reach a T-junction. Turn right, with care, along Market Street.

2. Turn second left along the A536, signposted to Ilminster and Ilchester, alongside the Victoria Hall, a large building on an island surrounded by the roads. Crewkerne is full of antique shops and you will pass Oscar's Antiques now on your left.

3. Continue straight up North Street which takes you towards the outskirts of Crewkerne, and at the top of a short hill turn left, the road being signposted to Merriott and Lopen.

4. Continue over the rise and down the other side to Merriott, and turn second right by the post office. This takes you through the back streets of Merriott where you will find pretty cottages built in golden Ham Stone from nearby Ham Hill. At the top of this street turn left into Church Street, signposted to Hinton St George and Ilminster, passing the King's Head pub on your right. There's a potter on your left on the corner and then you pass Merriott church on your right. Turn right along Sandy Hole Lane.

5. This narrow lane takes you down to flatter ground past Sockety Farm before rising gently through the apple orchards of Over Stratton. Cycle through the village past the Royal Oak pub to a T-junction with a main road.

6. Turn left, and then almost immediately right. Take care here, the traffic travels fast down the hill towards you. You now turn right again to cross the A303 (once the Roman Fosse Way) on a bridge. Turn right after the bridge and roll down into South Petherton, turning left at a T-junction at the end of South Street. This brings you into the centre of this very attractive village where there are two cafés should you require refreshment. From the centre of the village turn right, signposted to East Lambrook and Martock.

7. At the T-junction (car park on the right), turn left and continue out of South Petherton. Roll down the slope and take the first left, signposted to East Lambrook. Follow this lane into the village where you will find East Lambrook Manor Garden, created by Margery Fish, on your left.

8. On the right is the Rose and Crown pub, but be strong and fork left to the hamlet of New Cross. At the T-junction turn left in New Cross past the thatched white house, then immediately right by the post

box. This attractive lane climbs gently up onto Burrow Hill, visible for miles around as a neat cone topped with a tree. Continue until you meet the T-junction in Burrow, ignoring the turn to Lake Farm.

9. Turn right along the road signposted to Burrow Hill Cider, uphill for a quarter of a mile until you see the entrance to Burrow Hill Cider Farm on the right. Enjoy your visit but go steady on the tasting!

10. Turn right out from the farm and continue down Burrow Hill into Stembridge. At the junction by the Rusty Axe pub turn left and carry straight on to Kingsbury Episcopi. If by now you are getting hungry, try the Wyndham Arms in Kingsbury, a beautiful old pub with a Cyclists Touring Club winged-wheel sign on its frontage.

11. Continue through Kingsbury Episcopi to pass a tiny lockup on the village green on your left. You pass through the village of Thorney and approach Muchelney. Stop to visit John Leach's Pottery on your right. Continue into Mulcheney, where the church, with its early 17th century painted ceiling, the Priest's House and the Abbey ruins are
   • worth a visit.

12. By the church turn left to Drayton, signposted Drayton and Curry Rivel, across the Levels. In Drayton continue with the Drayton Arms on the left and the church on your right. Go straight on across crossroads to the village of Curry Rivel. (That's unless you are seeking a shorter day ride. In this case, turn left here and continue until a T-junction with the B3168. Turn left to Hambridge and Westport where you pick up the main route again as described in paragraph 24.

13. When you meet the main road through Curry Rivel (A378) turn left, signposted to Taunton, then right at the Bell Hotel. This smaller road takes you through the back streets of Curry Rivel. Continue straight on past the church until you meet a T-junction.

14. Turn left and proceed along this lane to the hamlet of Heale and as the road starts a steep descent look out for a metal National Trust signpost on your right which says "Red Hill". Descend Red Hill with Care! It has a spectacularly distracting view as you come down onto West Sedge Moor. Beware traffic climbing the hill towards you.

15. Continue until you meet a high railway bridge and a T-junction. Turn left, signposted Stathe and Burrowbridge, alongside the embanked River Parrett, to the village of Stathe. In Stathe, turn left, signposted Stoke St Gregory and North Curry. After crossing the railway again, turn left as signposted to Stoke St Gregory, past a red 'phone box, which will bring you down the hill to Stoke St Gregory. Cycle on until you reach the Rose and Crown pub on your right. It is

well-known for its food and bed and breakfast accommodation, and may well be your planned overnight stop.

16. If, however, you would like a slightly longer day, continue to ride by the Rose and Crown. Follow the road past the church with its fine octagonal tower and through the village centre. The road leaves the village. After passing a post office on your left turn right at Meare Green sign (by a red brick house on the corner) into a lane named Curload.

17. Pass by the English Basket and Hurdle Centre on the right. Cycle through Curload and over the railway line into the village of Altheney, site of King Alfred the Great's monastery and cake burning exploits. Continue to a T-junction and turn left towards Burrow bridge. As you cross the bridge over the River Parrett again, there is a good view of Burrow Mump, crowned by its church, on the right.

18. At the T-junction turn right into Burrowbridge, go over the bridge and turn immediately left alongside the river. Turn right, as signposted to Thorngrove and Middlezoy, onto Earlake Moor which is a very beautiful place with good views back to Burrow Mump. When you arrive in the hamlet of Thorngrove, turn right at the T-junction towards Middlezoy.

19. Just as you come into Middlezoy, take a right turn into a lane named Holloway which takes you across Nether Moor. At a T-junction turn left onto the A361 which runs through the village of Othery, a village blessed with two excellent bed and breakfast places. Both are on the main road in the middle of the village.

20. If you are staying in Othery retrace yesterday's route back to Curload. Here, you pass the English Basket and Hurdle Centre again and at the T-junction at the top of a small hill turn right towards the village of Meare Green. Look out for a huge wicker basket suspended beside the road on your right. This is the Willows and Wetlands Visitor Centre. Those staying in Stoke St Gregory should cycle out of Stoke past the church with the octagonal tower until you reach the Willows and Wetlands Visitor Centre at Meare Green.

21. On leaving the Centre turn right and continue to North Curry. Turn left, as signposted to Helland. It's downhill most of the way and onto the south end of West Sedge Moor, which stretches away on your left. Follow the lane across the Levels to Listoke, ignoring a dead end turn on the right on a corner. Continue until you reach a T-junction with the A378.

22. Turn left and climb up the hill through the trees on the A378, taking care because of faster traffic here. You are looking for a sharp right

turn, signposted Beercrocombe, Curry Mallet and Hatch Beauchamp. Take the first left turn off this lane, signposted to Curry Mallet and Beercrocombe. This takes you downhill to a T-junction.

23. Turn left here, the road being signposted to Fivehead. Continue to St Albans Farm where you turn first right. At the next T-junction turn left, no signpost. Go to the next T-junction (which is a crossroads if you count the track leading off opposite you) where you turn right. This lane leads along between willow trees, crossing Fivehead River and then the River Isle before coming into the village of Isle Brewers with its unusual tiled church spire.

24. Continue straight on out of Isle Brewers until you reach a T-junction with the B3168 road at the village of Westport. Turn right and then first left, signposted to Barrington. Cycle on down this lane until you reach the staggered crossroads in Barrington village, by the playing field. Turn left through this pretty village towards Barrington Court.

25. Continue out of the village and when you reach a crossroads, turn left to Shepton Beauchamp where the Duke of York pub might well be an appropriate lunch stop. Leave Shepton on the lane past the Fives Court and at the crossroads turn left, signposted to Crewkerne. This lane will cross the A303 (the Fosse Way again) on a bridge. Take the next right downhill into the village of Seavington St Michael, marked "Except for Access". Seavington St Michael is actually signposted straight on. Don't!

26. At the T-junction with the busier road through the village turn right past the Volunteer pub, then next left, signposted Seavington St Mary. Cycle down this lane and turn second left, after the post box. The landscape begins to roll here! Climb the low rise of Easterdown Hill and at the T-junction turn left.

27. You are now on a narrow, bumpy lane known as Furzy Knaps. Follow it down to the T-junction with the Fosse Way, which here is a beautiful Somerset lane and an obvious Roman Road. The T-junction is marked by a handsome copper beech tree. Turn right along the old Fosse way until you reach the village of Dinnington. If the Rose and Crown is open, call in to get to the bottom of the history of the Dinnington Docks and Railway . . . the beer is good too.

28. Continue through Dinnington. You will notice the road turning up the hill and the sides of the banks, thick with trees, rising above it as befitting such an ancient hollow way. Take the first left and ride along this lane, which winds and clambers along the ridge to the picturesque village of Hinton St George.

29. In the centre of the village you pass the Poulett Arms pub on your

left, and come immediately to a crossroads. Take a right turn into South Street. This little lane hurtles off downhill, round a sharp bend and then up again. At the top of the short climb turn left, signposted to Merriott and Crewkerne.

30. This lane runs along the ridge for a while, but has many bends - so listen for traffic. At a crossroads known as Shutteroaks continue straight over towards Crewkerne. The lane now becomes very narrow, flying downhill and round a sharp bend by a cottage named The Haunted House. It then climbs steeply before another wild plunge down and up which brings you to Abbey Street in Crewkerne where the beautiful Perpendicular parish church can be seen to the right.

31. When you leave Crewkerne for the railway station you need to fork left at the end of Market Street, which is signposted to Dorchester. Continue out of town to rise up to the station.

GREAT CYCLING IDEAS!

The South West has witnessed increasing provision for cyclists in recent years with several county cycleways, and paths provided and even more being planned. There is one slight concern expressed about riding through the back lanes in Cornwall and Devon as they are often winding (therefore, have poor sight lines) and narrow. The worry is that cars might be travelling along them faster than they ought. So, it is argued that for our own safety we should not be using them. More is the pity for many of these back routes introduce you to idyllic countryside. If you ride defensively (i.e. listen hard and ease right up on tight corners) then these lanes are a marvellous introduction to the area. Cyclists could be encouraged and cars calmed here!

Avon

Avon Cycleway: an interesting 80-mile route which is waymarked throughout. There is a superb section between Portishead, Clevedon and Saltford and another between Mangotsfield, Chipping Sodbury and Thornbury. Leaflet available.

Bristol and Bath Railway Path: for a taste of this excellent 13-mile path between Bath and Bristol, see Philip Insall's route at the beginning of this chapter. Leaflet available.

Leisure Rides in Avon: This series of leaflets offers suggestions for exploring some of the county's loveliest corners, including rides into the Mendips, Severn Vale and Berkeley from local railheads. 12 routes available at local tourist information centres; price range £3 - £4.

Cornwall

Camel Trail, Padstow to Bodmin and Wenfordbridge: Probably one of the most popular all-year trails in the UK, where you will find nearly as many out on a mild Boxing Day as on a summer's day. Fifteen miles of sheer bliss!

Camelford Old Station: The Museum of Historic Cycling. Tel: (01840) 212811 before travelling.

Cardinham Woods, near Bodmin: four to five miles off-road through pleasant woodland.

South East Cornwall: *Six Cycle Guides Exploring South East Cornwall.* Great introduction to the back lanes of the area. Price £2-3 from local tourist information centres.

Devon

Devon Circular Cycle Route: a 260-mile route devised by Bryan Cath at Combe Lodge Hotel, Ilfracombe. Ideal for a week's holiday - see Cycle Holiday listing.

Exe Cycle Route, Exeter: a 4-mile ride through Exeter near to the River Exe. There is also a series of lovely rides out of Exeter provided by Saddles and Paddles.

Plym Valley Path, Plymouth to Goodameavy: the only off-road route into Dartmoor starting at the Laira Bridge at Plymouth although Sustrans has provided a link into the city. Very scenic including woodland at Bickleigh Vale.

West Devon Cycle Routes: there are three in the series so far inviting you to follow country lanes to historic villages, Devon tea rooms and welcoming inns. They are all worth cycling but the Bere Peninsula ride offers spectacular views: Bere Peninsula 9 miles, Sticklepath 30 miles, Tavistock 26 miles. Leaflets are available.

Tarka Trail: running along the route between Braunton - Barnstaple - Bideford - Taw Valley for 15 miles, this "green tourism" development *par excellence* encourages people to walk and cycle in an area made famous by Henry Williamson's book, "Tarka the Otter". The Tarka Trail introduces the cyclist to the world of Tarka.

There are also much hillier routes criss-crossing North Devon beyond Ilfracombe, which are fine once you've limbered up on the trails. The same applies to the Honiton area.

Dorset

Castleman Trailway, near Upton: an off-road route between Upton to the River Avon near Ringwood. A walking and cycling path which will hopefully connect (when complete) with a similar route from Poole.

Cycling in West Dorset: a cycling pack offering The Great West Dorset Cycle Ride (65 miles) and a series of shorter routes: *Cycling in and around Beaminster, 16 miles; Cycling in and around Dorchester, 16 miles; Cycling in and around Sherborne, 15 miles*

These rides cover the ground worshipped by novelist and poet, Thomas Hardy, taking the rider to the thatched village of Abbotsbury, to the Cerne Valley to see the notorious giant and to historic towns such as Bridport, Beauminster and Sherborne. Small charge per leaflet. Tel: West Dorset Tourist Information on (01305) 267992.

Dorset Cycle Guide: The guide covers cycling opportunities throughout the county including Purbeck, Corfe Castle, Blackmore Vale and the villages of East Dorset. Packed with details for the would be cyclist including refreshment stops, accommodation and up to the minute information on cycle hire. Contact Dorset Tourism on (01202) 221001.

East Dorset Cycle Route: A route which links Bournemouth and Poole to surrounding villages and towns. 62 miles of leisure cycling on 'B' and 'C' roads mainly which will join the Vale and Downs cycleway in North Dorset.

Purbeck Cycleway: This 55-mile cycleway offers a figure-of-eight route based on Corfe Castle through heathland, chalk ridge and downland as well as Wareham Forest. It runs through several ancient villages in Purbeck and there are shorter loops of 12, 26 and 27 miles ideal for day excursions.

Vale and Downs Cycleway: Also known as the North Dorset Cycleway this exceptional route passes through Blackmore Vale, the Dorset Downs and Cranborne Chase, all of which are known for their outstanding natural beauty. The cycleway is waymarked between villages and into the characterful towns of Blandford and Shaftesbury.

Corfe Castle, Dorset (Dorset Tourism)

Somerset

Cycling in South Somerset: a 100-mile waymarked on-road cycle route through a superb part of South Somerset. Leaflet available. Also try National Trust Centenary Cycle Rides.

Mendip Cycle Routes: Leaflet available.

Somerset County Council Routes: Leaflets describing great rides through Somerset available from local tourist information offices. For example *The Avalon Marches.*

Wiltshire

Cycling in The Wiltshire Downs: Leaflet on cycling the by-ways of the Downs including Giants Grave and white horses.

Trails for Mountain Bikes: *Cycling Over The Marlborough Downs* is explained in a leaflet illustrating bridleway and tracks suitable for mountain bikes.

Swindon to Marlborough Railway Path and Cycle Route: a Sustrans route out of Swindon on the old Midland and South West Junction railway, currently extending 6 miles. For access from Swindon, use the Swindon Cycle Route Network map.

Wiltshire Cycleway: a 160-mile route, but there are also shorter circular loops suggested from this County waymarked way, for example between Horningsham and Salisbury.

Cycle Holiday Companies

Adventure Cycles, 2 Snows Cottages, Mamhead, Exeter EX6 8HW. Tel: (01626) 864786. Cycling Holidays available.

Bike Tours Ltd, PO Box 75, Bath, BA1 1BX. Open: all year. Tel: (01225) 480130. A major organiser of bike events. Send for holiday brochure.

Combe Lodge Hotel, Chambercombe Park, Ifracombe, Devon EX34 9QP. Open: all year. Tel: (01271) 864518. Self-guided holiday breaks in North Devon. Bring own bike or CH available. Itineraries supplied plus transport to starting points. Proprietor is the author of *Devon Cycle Tour.*

Cycle Power, 2 Broadmoor Road, Corfe Mullen, Wimbourne, Dorset BH21 3RA. Open: all year. Self-guided tours. Tel (01202) 691279.

Devizes Bikes, Pinecroft, Potterne Road, Devises SN10 5DA. Open: all year. Tel: (01380) 721433. Holidays in Wiltshire.

Level Pedalling, Chapel Cottage, Court Mill, Merriott, Somerset TA16 5NL. Open: March to October. Tel: (01460) 72156. Great self-guided and bespoke short-break holidays.

Rockvale Mountain Bike Hire, Rockvale, Lustleigh, near Newton Abbot, TQ13 9TH. Open: all year. Tel: (016477) 264. Holidays through Dartmoor and Devon. CH available.

Roots West, Avalon, Brea Farm, St Buryan, Lands End, Cornwall TR19 6JB. Open: all year. Tel: (01736) 871876. Self-led and guided tours.

Rough Tracks, 6 Castle Street, Calne SN11 ODU. Open: all year. Tel: (01249) 817723. Plus overseas holidays.

Saddles and Paddles, 21 The Cellars, The Quayside, Exeter. Open: April to December. Tel: (01392) 424241. Offering holiday breaks in Devon. CH available plus local rides. BR.

Somerset Cycling, Ash Farm, Pineapple Lane, Salway Ash, near Bridport, DT6 5HY. Open: all year. Tel: (01308) 488465. Self-guided tours in Devon, Dorset and Somerset.

Somerset Handlebar Tours, 8 Wick Hollow, Glastonbury, Somerset BA6 8JJ. Tel: (01458) 834244.

Spokes Cycle Tours, Fairfield House, The Street, Didmarton, Badminton, Avon GL9 1DS. Open: Tel: (01454) 238199. Tours in SW and Cotswolds.

Wessex Wheels, Broadstone Barn, Walditch, Bridport, Dorset DT6 4LA. Open: all year. Tel: (01308) 427430. Guided and self-guided tours, short breaks in and around Dorset.

Cycle Hire Companies

Avon:

Bath: *Avon Valley Cyclery*, "Underneath the Arches", Arch 37, rear of Bath Spa Station, Bath BA1 1SX. Open: all year. Tel: (01225) 461880. BR; *City Cycles*, 6 Monmouth Place. Open: April to October. Tel: (01225) 311595. BR.

Weston-super-Mare: *W.h.e.e.l*, The Garage, Main Road, Hutton, near Weston BS24 9QQ. Open: all year. Tel: (01934) 811112.

Cornwall:

Bodmin: *Glynn Valley Cycle Hire*, Cardinam Woods, Margate, Bodmin. Open: Daily from June to September, Easter and Bank Holidays & Suns. Tel: (01208) 74244.

Bude: *North Coast Cycles*, Flexbury Garage, Ocean View Road, Bude EX23 8NH. Open: all year. Tel: (01288) 352974.

Camborne: *Aldridge Cycles*, 38 Cross Street, TR14 8EX. Open: all year. Tel: (01209) 714970. BR.

Launceston: *South West Cycles*, Lewannick House, Hurdon Road, PL15 9HW Open: all year. Tel: (01566) 772706.

Liskeard: *Liskeard Cycles*, Pig Meadow Lane, The Parade, Liskeard. Open: Summer only. Tel: (01579) 347696. BR.

Newquay: *Cycle Revolution*, 7 Beach Road, Newquay, TR7 1ES. Open: May to October Tel: (01637) 872364. BR; *Hutton Hire Supplies*, The Old Store, Trevemper Hill Lane, Newquay, TR8 4QD. Open: all year. Tel: (01637) 851801. BR.

Penzance: *Geoff's Bikes*, Victoria Place, Penzance, TR18 4DB. Open: all year. Tel: (01736) 63665. BR.

Redruth: *Bike Chain*, 82 Mount Ambrose, Redruth. Open: all year. Tel: (01209) 215270. BR.

Truro: *Trail and Trek*, 36 Fore Street, Chacewater, Truro, TR4 8PT. Open: all year. Tel: (01872) 561124. BR; *Truro Cycles*, 110 Kenwyn Street, Truro, TR1 3DJ. BR. Open: all year. Tel: (01872) 71703. 'Phone first to book. BR.

Wadebridge: *Bridge Bike Hire*, The Camel Trail, Wadebridge, Cornwall, PL27 7AL. Open: all year. Tel: (01208) 813050; *Cycle Revolutions*, Eddystone Road, PL27 1XL. Open: all year. Tel: (01208) 812021.

Devon:

Barnstaple: *Tarka Trail Cycle Hire*, British Rail Station, EX21 2AY. Open: Easter to October. Tel: (01271) 24202.

Bideford: *Bideford Bicycle Hire*, Torrington Street, East The Water, Bideford, EX39 4DR. Open: all year. Tel: (01237) 424123.

Braunton: *Swan Cycle Hire*, 6 The Square, Braunton, EX33 1JD. Open: all year. Tel: (01271) 815775.

Chulmleigh: *Eggesford Country Centre*, Eggesford Gardens, Eggesford, EX18 7QU. Open: all year. Tel: (01769) 580250.

Exeter: *Mark Partridge Cycles*, Gissons House, Kennford, Nr Exeter, EX6 7UD. Open: April to October. Tel: (01392) 833303. *Flash Gordon/StDavids Hire*,Preston's Yard, Ludwell Lane, Wonford, EX25 AQ. Tel: (01329) 213141.

Honiton: *Cycle (Honiton)*, Lanson House, King Street, Honiton, EX14 8AA. Open: April-September. Tel: (01404) 47211. BR.

Ilfracombe: *Tors Mountain Bike Hire*, 30 Salther Close, EX34 8LY. Open: all year. Tel: (01271) 866886.

Kingsbridge: *Kingsbridge Hire Centre*, Old Railway Yard, Kingsbridge, TQ7 1ES. Open: March to November. Tel: (01548) 853679.

North Tawton: *Dartmoor Cycle Hire*, 68 Fore Street, EX20 2DT. Open: all year. Tel: (01837) 82685. Tours too.

Plymouth: *Action Sports*, Queen Anne's Battery, Coxside, PL4 OLP. Open: all year. Tel: (01752) 268328. BR; *Alltrax,* Star Garage, Down Thomas, PL9 0AR. Open: all year. Tel: (01752) 863272.

Tavistock: *Tavistock Cycles Ltd*, Paddons Row, Brook Street, PL19 OHF. Open: all year. Tel: (01822) 617630.

Teignmouth: *Mylor Cycles*, 10 Northumberland Place, Teignmouth, TQ14 8DD. Open: all year. Tel: (016267) 78460. BR.

Tiverton: *Maynards Cycle Shop*, 25 Gold Street, Tiverton, EX16 6QB. Open: March to October. Tel: (01884) 253979.

Torquay: *Colin Lewis Cycles,* 15 East Street, Torre, Torquay. Open: March-Sept. Tel: (01803) 25176. BR.

Totnes: *Recycle*, Old Stonemason's, South Street, Totnes TQ9 5DZ. Open: all year. Tel: (01803) 867214. BR.

Dorset:

Blandford: *Jack Hearnes*, 38 Salisbury St, DT11 7PR. Open: All Year. Tel: (01747) 825757.

Dorchester: *Dorchester Cycles*, 31 Great Western Road, DT1 1UF. Open: all year. Tel: (01305) 268787. BR.

Gillingham: *Wheels*, Station Rd. Open: All Year. Tel: (01747) 825757. BR.

Poole: *Bikes (Branksome)*, 431-433 Poole Road. Open: all year. Tel: (01202) 769202; *Purbeck Mountain Biking*, Corner Croft, Purbeck Road, Lychett Matravers, BH16 6EN. Open: all year. Tel: (01202) 623516. BR (Branksome).

Stalbridge: *Dorset Cycles*, High Street, DT10 2LL. Open: All year. Tel: (01963) 362476.

Weymouth: *Second Wind Watersports*, Overcombe Beach, Overcombe Corner, Preston, Weymouth, DT3 6PJ. Open: all year. Tel: (01305) 835301. BR. *Westham Cycles*, 128 Abbotsbury Road, DT4 OJT. Open: all year. Tel: (01305) 776977. BR.

Somerset:

Burnham-on-Sea: *G.H Cycles*, Adam Street, TA8 1PE. Open: all year. Tel: (01278) 782350.

Crowcombe: *Quantock Orchard Caravan Park*, TA4 4AW. Open: All season. Tel: (01984) 618618.

Glastonbury: *Pedallers*, 8 Magdalene Street, BA6 9EH. Open: Easter to September. Tel: (01458) 831117.

Highbridge: *Somerset Cycle Hire*, New Road Farm, East Huntspill, TAP 3P2. Open: April to Dec. Tel: (01278) 792777.

Minehead: *P.G Hayes Garages*, Mart Road Trading Estate, TA24 SBJ. Open: Summer only. Tel: (01643) 703461.

Taunton: *Ralph Coleman Cycles*, 79 Station Rd. Open: All year. Tel: (01823) 275622.

Yeovil: *Yeovil Cycle Centre*, 8-10 South Western Terrace. Open: all year. Tel: (01935) 22000. BR.

Wiltshire:

Bradford on Avon: *The Lock Inn Cottage*, Canal-side Tea Gardens, 48 Frome Road, BA15 1LE. Open: all year. Tel: (01225) 868068. BR.

Devizes: *M.J. Hiscock Cycles*, 59 Northgate Street. Open: all year, but not Sun afternoons. Tel: (01380) 722236.

Marlborough: *Rentall*, Pelham Yard, London Road. Open: all year. Tel: (01672) 513028; *Savernake Forest Hotel*, Burbage, SN8 3AY. Open: all year. Tel: (01672) 810206.

Salisbury: *Hayball & Co*, 26-30 Winchester Street. Open: all year. Tel: (01722) 411378. BR.

Swindon: *Leisure Cycles*, 51 Devizes Road, Old Town. Open: all year. Tel: (01793) 432476. BR.

SOUTHERN ENGLAND

Includes Berkshire, Buckinghamshire, Hampshire, Isle of Wight, Oxfordshire (for Dorset, see the West Country)
Tourist Information: Southern Tourist Board,
40 Chamberlyne Road, Eastleigh, SO5 5JH.
Tel: (01703) 620006

The Southern Tourist Board region looks like an elongated strip which runs from the golden stone villages of Oxfordshire and Buckinghamshire down to the Hampshire Coast. Oxfordshire is a splendid gateway to the eastern corners of the Cotswolds, through charming towns such as honey-coloured Charlbury, or Hook Norton with its traditional Victorian brewery. Others might travel on the Oxfordshire Cycleway to Witney and through the Windrush valley.

The City of Oxford is steeped in history and it is easy to tour the ancient colleges by bike although the traffic can be heavy and visitors are thick on the ground.

Buckinghamshire and Berkshire allow access to the forested arc of the Chiltern Hills and the Thames Valley. It is busier than Oxfordshire but there are pockets of countryside which warrant a little saunter. Hampshire brings you to the North and South Downs, chalk upland areas which are accessible in places to cyclists although the pressures to balance conservation with use are constant.

There also are routes to be plotted between Winchester and Petersfield through the Meon Valley or farther south along the fringes of The New Forest. Speed limits are restricted in many parts of the forest to 40 mph and it is possible to deviate from main routes onto the made up tracks but make sure that you keep to the permissible tracks. A short hop across the Solent Water brings the cyclist to the Isle of Wight, once referred to as the Cyclists' island, and welcoming still the off-road and touring cyclist. The main roads are busy in summer but journey away from these and the island is yours.

This region is busier than other parts of England because of the proximity of Greater London. This should not deter the cyclist from aiming for the many splendid destinations on hand such as The New Forest or Oxfordshire where cycling away from fumes offers a real breath of fresh air.

COUNTRYSIDE RIDE

The New Forest

Susan Achmatowicz of Country Lanes

Distance: 34 miles.

Terrain: An easy-going day ride but a mountain bike or hybrid would be preferable for the morning section.

Maps: O.S. Landranger 184 and 185 or O.S Outdoor Leisure 22.

Rail Access: 'Country Lanes' (see later) offer a special day package for those arriving at Brockenhurst railway station by train.

Accommodation and Refreshment: there is accommodation at the Sandy Ball Holiday Centre and also in Fordingbridge. The nearest youth hostel is at Burley several miles away. There are several pubs on the route which cater well for the cyclist. Contact Tourist Information at Fordingbridge (April to September only) on (01425) 654560.

Cycle Hire and Holidays: call Country Lanes on (01425) 655022.

The Ride

This is a ride of contrasts, a morning spent riding through the glades of the New Forest and across open heathland where ponies, deer and sheep roam at will. Many cyclists are intrigued to find that less than half of the New Forest is actually under wood. The name "forest" emanates from medieval times when royalty chose large tracts of land for hunting purposes. For centuries this was the haunt of kings and queens and their entourage of nobility. It was the strict law of the Forest that has conserved so much and, to this day, special laws survive from a time when William the Conqueror proclaimed it as Nova Foresta.

The afternoon loop is different, for the Avon Valley route runs through villages, many with thatched cottages and rich in heritage, to the small town of Fordingbridge where Georgian houses back up to its Early English church.

Seeing Places

Breamore House: Breamore House dates from Elizabethan times but much of the building we see today was rebuilt in the late 1850s after a disastrous fire. There is now a museum in the old stable block and in the grounds stands an exceptional Saxon church.

Rockbourne Roman Villa: this can be found near to the homely village of Rockbourne, described by the legendary architectural writer Pevsner as "one of the prettiest in Hampshire". The ruins of the Roman villa were evidently found during the Second World War by an amateur archaelogist. The museum here contains many finds from subsequent excavations and it is worth parking the bike for an hour or two to explore the remains, if only to view one of the finest courtyard mosaics in England.

The first part of the ride offers a considerable amount of off-road cycling using Forestry Commission approved tracks. The terrain is mostly rolling hills with one short sharp climb at Blissford. The Avon Valley loop is mainly flat and along quiet country lanes with two short grades, one at Castle Hill and the other on the approach to Godshill.

Cycling in the New Forest (Country Lanes)

44

The Route

1. From the entrance of Sandy Balls turn left to ride through Godshill, over a cattle-grid, by the Fighting Cocks inn. Ride through heathland on the B3078 up Deadmans Hill to pass a junction with the B3080 coming in from the left.

2. At the cross roads sign on the left, turn right to join a gravel track. The gate along the track is identifiable with the lettering B13 on the left-hand side. Pass Eyeworth Pond (also called Iron Wells due to its chalybeate properties), on your right. Look out for the ducks!

3. At the T-junction with the tarmac road, turn left to ascend the hill. At the top, turn right to enter Fritham car park. Keep straight on here for about 200 metres if you seek refreshment at the Royal Oak Inn.

4. Otherwise, at the fork in the track, go straight on through the car park. At the gate with the words "Forestry Commission Car Free Area: Access Limited" and the lettering B8 near to the hinge, go straight on, through the gate into the Forest again.

5. About a mile on you come to a fork in the track with a small triangle of grass. Go straight on here. You drop to a brook and pass by Holly Hatch Cottage on your left. The track curves left into Holly Hatch Enclosure. At the cross roads with another track turn right.

6. At the fork in the track, veer right. Pass through a gate (closing it behind you). In less than a mile you come to a double gate. Go straight on. Please close the gate behind you. Pass through a single gate and enter Woodford Bottom car park.

7. At the T-junction turn right. Do not turn off this track. Join a tarmac road and cross the ford. At the T-junction with the Red Shoot Inn on your left, turn right. Follow this road to a crossroads where you go right on the road signposted to Mockbeggar and North Gorley. Cross the ford and pass by Moyles Court School on the left.

8. A mile farther, at the fork in the road, veer right as signposted to Furze Hill. Where the road turns sharp left and crosses the river, with Fir Tree Farm Equestrian Centre on your right, veer right onto a tarmac road. There is a rectangular blue, red and white "Dead End" sign on the left of the road.

9. At the fork in the track veer left as signposted to the car park. Pass the car park on your right and cross the ford. Beware of the holes! At the T-junction at the end of Blissford Road, turn right to head back to Godshill.

10. The second part of the loop turns left after crossing the cattle grid and just before the Fighting Cocks pub. The road is signposted to

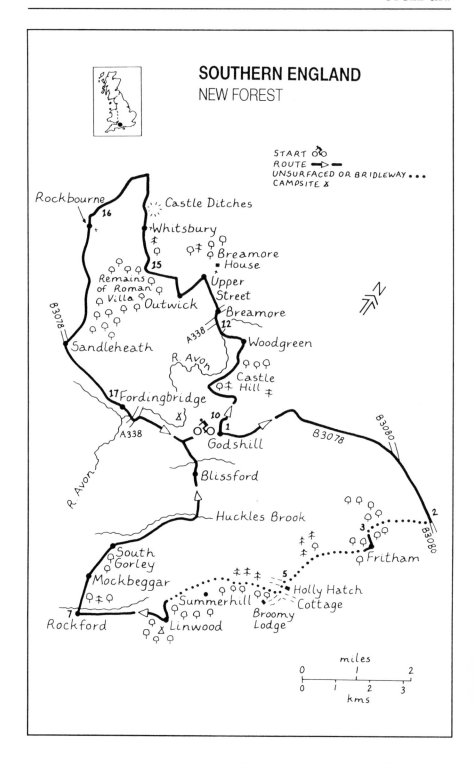

SOUTHERN ENGLAND
NEW FOREST

START �
ROUTE ➡️
UNSURFACED OR BRIDLEWAY ...
CAMPSITE ✗

Rockbourne
16
Castle Ditches
Whitsbury
Breamore House
15
Remains of Roman Villa
Outwick
Upper Street
Breamore
B3078
A338
Sandleheath
R. Avon
12
Woodgreen
Castle Hill
17 Fordingbridge
10
1
A338
Godshill
B3078
B3080
R. Avon
Blissford
Huckles Brook
2
3
Fritham
B3080
South Gorley
Mockbeggar
Holly Hatch Cottage
5
Summerhill
Broomy Lodge
7
Rockford
Linwood

miles
0   1   2
0   1   2   3
kms

46

Woodgreen. After Godshillwood Farm, veer left at the fork in the road signposted to Castle Hill. You pass by benches on the left along this section where there are extensive views across the Avon valley. Castle Hill is what remains of a motte and bailey fortress.

11. At the edge of Woodgreen, turn left at the T-junction to enter the village. At the T-junction with "Ye Olde Shop" on your left, turn left. Cross the River Avon bridge and pass the old mill on your right.

12. At the T-junction with the main A338 road turn right (signposted to Salisbury) into Breamore. At the next junction, with Breamore Post Office on your left, turn left along the road signposted to Breamore Church and House. At the fork in the road veer right, signposted to Breamore House. At the crossroads, go straight over, signposted to Breamore Church.

13. At the crossroads, with the entrance to Breamore House in front of you turn right to visit the church and turn left to leave bikes near the toilets, tea rooms and the Countryside Museum before exploring Breamore House. Exit the Breamore House property via the car park.

14. Turn right onto the minor road and follow this around a sharp left-hand bend. Pass a red telephone box on your left. At the crossroads, turn right to enter the road with the 6'6" road width restriction signposted to Whitsbury.

15. Follow the road around the left-hand bend and ascend the hill. At the next junction turn right, signposted to Whitsbury. At the T-junction turn right, signposted Whitsbury. Pass through the village with the Cartwheel Inn on the right-hand side. At the fork in the road veer left, signposted to Rockbourne and Damerham.

16. This runs along the edge of Dunberry Hill to Rockbourne where you turn left into the village. Pass Little Duff's Rose and Thistle inn on your right, and then the entrance to Rockbourne Roman Museum on your right. The road runs through to a crossroads at Sandleheath where you turn left onto the B3078 to Fordingbridge. Pass the Load of Hay inn on your left.

17. At the roundabout in the town, turn right on the road signposted to Ringwood (A338). Pass by the sports ground and the George Inn on the right. Cross the River Avon and go under the A338. Return to Sandy Balls at Godshill.

GREAT CYCLING IDEAS!

There are several off-road cycling opportunities including parts of The Ridgeway which runs through Berkshire and Oxfordshire, and the Oxfordshire Cycleway. To the south are the New Forest and the Isle of Wight, both of which offer great promise.

Walkers and cyclists with the Ridgeway Explorer (Ridgeway Project)

Berkshire

The Ridgeway: This follows an ancient way for 85 miles from East Kennett to Berkshire where it meets the Icknield way at Ivinghoe near Tring. Runs through the Chilterns in Berkshire. All sections in this county open to cyclists. Check when planning a ride along other parts by contacting the Ridgeway Officer, Countryside Service, Dept of Leisure and Arts, Holton, Oxfordshire OX9 1QQ.

Buckinghamshire

Buckinghamshire Circular Rides: the County Council has initiated a series of circular rides, of which there are separate leaflets including: *Bledow Circular Ride through the Chilterns; Hanslope Circular Ride,*etc They vary from 10 to 20 miles in length through gently undulating countryside.

Midshires Way: a 225 mile route which, for the most part, follows public bridleways on quiet country lanes. The route varies from county to county. The very last section into Stockport from the Peak District is not available for cyclists so as yet it is difficult to ride the entire route. Leaflets available.

Swans Way: this 65 mile bridle-route from Goring-on-Thames in the south of the county to Salcey Forest in the north is available to cyclists but can be hard going in wet weather.

Three Shires Way: a 37-mile long bridleway running from Tathall End to Grafham Water in Cambridgeshire. Again the emphasis is on providing for horse riders and the route can become messy after rain.

Hampshire

Meon Valley: in the west of the county there are several lovely rides in the Meon valley using the Soberton Way.

New Forest: the New Forest is by far the best cycling patch in Hampshire where you can escape trafficked roads. There are nearly as many miles of made up forest tracks but cyclists are restricted so check local information and endeavour to follow the New Forest Cycling Code which is available as a leaflet.

Off Road Cycle Trails: a water resistant pocket-sized pack of 12 self-guided routes, 3-26 miles long through Hampshire's countryside. Price: about £3.

Queen Elizabeth Country Park, Waterlooville: the Country Park has set out a special mountain bike route which is ideal for beginners, something which should be happening throughout the UK.

Southampton Cyclists Guide: a leaflet detailing cycle routes and facilities in and around Southampton. Small charge.

Isle of Wight

By-ways and Bridleways by Mountain Bike: a set of fold-out leaflets illustrating many routes on the island produced by the County Council with Sponsorship from the Countryside Commission and Offshore Sports. Price range: £3 - £4.

Cowes to Newport cycle path: a 4-mile off-road route between the port and centre of the island.

Oxfordshire

Cycle Tours in Oxfordshire: this is a series of cheap and cheerful booklets outlining tours through Oxfordshire villages. Price: about £1.

Cycle into Oxford: a fold-up leaflet (small charge) which is geared primarily for commuters but is useful for the leisure cyclist.

Oxfordshire Circular Rides: a series of leaflets featuring bridleways. Contact Countryside Service on (01865) 810226.

Oxfordshire Cycleway: a 200-mile cycle route which runs through the eastern fringes of the Cotswolds as well as the Chilterns. There are link routes in and out of Oxford to allow access to the circular ride. Small charge for very good fold out leaflet.

Cycle Holiday Companies

Country Lanes, 9 Shaftesbury Street, Fordingbridge, Hampshire SP6 1JF Open: all year. Tel: (01425) 655022; Self-guided and guided tours available from this quality company. Cycle Hire also available from Sandy Balls Holiday Centre, Fordingbridge.

"Straw Hat" Camping and Cycling Holidays, 12 College Road, Newport, Isle of Wight, PO30 1BH. Camping and cycling holidays on the island during June through to August. Cycle Hire available all year. Tel: (01983) 528820.

Cycle Hire Companies

Berkshire:

Newbury: *Rentall,* Hambridge Road, Newbury RG14 5SS. Open: all year. Tel: (01635) 31276. BR.

Slough: *Stows,* 1 Old Crown, Windsor Road, Slough SL1 2DJ. Open: all year. Tel: (01753) 520528. BR.

Thatcham: *M.J. Muttram,* Unit 4, Green Lane Industrial Estate RG13 4RG. Open: all year (but one week's notice required from October to March). Tel: (01635) 868740. BR.

Windsor: *Windsor Cycle Hire,*50 The Arches, Alma Road, SL4 1QZ. Open: all year. Tel: (01753) 830220. BR.

Buckinghamshire:

Marlow: *Saddle Safari,* Old Slaughterhouse, off Spittal Street, SL7 3HL. Open: Tuesday to Saturday all year and Sundays in summer. Tel: (01628) 477020. BR.

Princes Risborough: *David Bolton Cycles,* Lloyds Bank Garden, Market Square, HP17 OAN. Open: Tel: (01844) 345949. BR.

Hampshire:

Andover: *Bolton's Bikes and Tandems,* 8/8a Andover Road, Ludgershall, SP11 7LZ. Open: all year, closed Wed. and Sat. Tel: (01264) 791818. BR.

Fleet: *Bike 1,* PO Box 105, Fleet, Hampshire GU13 8R7. Open: all year. Tel: (01252) 624022. BR. Organisers of great day rides which are popular and Bike 1's reputation is growing year by year. The day rides are based mainly in the South and South East.

Aldershot: *Cycle Scene,* 48 Grosvenor Road, GU11 3DY. Open: all year. Tel: (01252) 25640. BR.

Brockenhurst: *New Forest Cycle Experience,* The Island Shop, Brookley Road, SO42 7RR. Open: all year. Tel: (01590) 624204. BR.

Gosport: *B. Osborne,* 80 Gregson Ave, Bridgemart, Gosport, PO13 OUR. Open: March to October. Tel: (01329) 822402. BR.

Lymington: *H.E. Figgures*, 122-124 High Street, SO41 9AQ. Open: all year. Tel: (01590) 672002 Holidays are also arranged April-October. BR.

Lyndhurst: *A.A. Bike Hire (New Forest)*, Fern Glen, Gosport Lane, SO43 7BL Open: all year. Tel: (01703) 283349.

New Milton: *Ashley Cycles*, 49 Ashley Road, BH25 6AZ. Open: all year. Tel: (01425) 618103. BR.

Southampton: *Cyclemania*, 50 Romsey Road, Shirley. Open: all year. Tel: (01703) 773323; *Peter Hargroves Cycles*, 453 Millbrook Road, Open: all year. Tel: (01703) 789160. BR; *The Cycle Shop*, Bridge Road, Park Gate SO3 7HG. Tel: (01289) 57249. BR.

Isle of Wight:

Cowes: *Cowes Cycle Hire*, 20 High Street, PO31 7TY. Open: April to October. Tel: (01983) 294910.

Sandown: *Sandown Tool Hire*, Unit 1, Senator Trading Estate, College Close, PO36 8EH. Open: Easter to October. Tel: (01983) 402396. BR.

Shanklin: *Offshore Sports*, 19 Orchardleigh Road, Shanklin, PO37 7NP. Open: all year. Tel: (01983) 866269. BR.

Ventnor: *Extreme Cycles*, Church Street, PO38 1SW. Open: all year. Tel: (01983) 852232.

Yarmouth: *Mobile Cycle Services*, 3 North View, Thorley, near Yarmouth, PO41 0SU. Open: all year, but please 'phone as bikes are not always available at the shop. Tel: (01983) 760818.

Oxfordshire:

Abingdon: *H & N Bragg Bikes Ltd*, 2 High Street, OX14 5AX. Open: March to September. Tel: (01235) 520034.

Banbury: *Trinder Bros*, 56-59 Broad Street, OX16 8BN. Open: all year. Tel: (01295) 262546. BR.

Oxford: *Cycle King*, 55 Walton Street, OXE 6AE. Open: all year. Tel: (01865) 516122; *Dentons Cycles*, 294 Banbury Road. Open: all year. Tel: (01865) 53859; *Penny Farthing Cycles*, 5 George Street, OX1 2AT. Open: all year. Tel: (01865) 249368; *Warlands Cycles*, 63 Botley Road, OX2 OB5. Open: all year. Tel: (01865) 241336. BR.

LONDON & SOUTH-EAST ENGLAND

Includes London, Kent, Surrey, East Sussex, West Sussex.
Tourist Information: London Tourist Board: 26 Grosvenor Gardens, SW1W 0DU. Tel: 0171 730 3450
S.E. England Tourist Board: The Old Brew House, Warwick Park, Tunbridge Wells, TN2 5TU. Tel: 01892 540766

Through the good work of the London Cycling Campaign, the capital city is slowly becoming more cycle-friendly for the visitor, although it is still a distinct pleasure to ride up to Westminster Abbey or Buckingham Palace on your bike rather than arriving by coach. More's the pity that very few MPs ride their cycles to the House of Parliament! Cycling alongside The Thames or on permitted routes through some of London's parks can be enjoyable but much of the city is heavily trafficked. The countryside stretching from the wooded hills of Surrey to the elegant Victorian seaside resorts of Kent and Sussex offers a far better prospect and you can be there in less than two hours on a train.

Surrey is a gently undulating county where wooded chalk downs fall to heathland and commons. Box and Leith Hill are perhaps the best loved beauty spots hereabouts and have been landmarks for centuries. The bridleways in these areas are well used for off-road cycling.

The coastal counties of Kent, East and West Sussex provide a range of rides: the rounded heights of The North and South Downs to the mysterious and flat Romney Marsh, and the gently undulating Garden of England. Oasts, hopyards, orchards and vineyards can be seen in these parts, also some of England's finest houses including Leeds Castle.

There are no County cycleways but there are several off-road routes available. These are found mainly in East and West Sussex. There are also several country lane routes in Sussex. More are planned for Kent which is an enchanting county when you can actually get away from intrusive motorways and trunk roads. Both Kent and Sussex were host to the Tour de France in 1994, only the second time in the history of this great race which usually involves 200 riders and an entourage of 4000 back-up people. Let us hope that more trails are blazed as a result of publicity stemming from this world event. Vive le Tour d'Angleterre!

COUNTRYSIDE RIDE

The South Downs Way

Distance: 10 miles.

Terrain: a Day Ride by mountain bike. It is strenuous in places.

Maps: O.S. 199 Eastbourne, Hastings and surrounding area.

Accommodation and Refreshment: ample accommodation in Eastbourne and Alfriston. There is a pub in Jevington too. Contact Tourist Information at Eastbourne on (01323) 411400.

Cycle Hire: Forest Cycle Hire, Seven Sisters Country Park. Tel: (01323) 870310.

Rail Access: Eastbourne, Berwick and Glynde if the ride is extended.

The Ride

This is a triumphant wheel along one of England's most ancient ways, ground which would certainly have been known to our tribal ancestors. Reminders of the past can be seen throughout the route but The Long Man near Wilmington, said to date from Iron Age times, is the most spectacular in the area. These chalk uplands are very precious and the South Downs Way is a tribute to those individuals and authorities who welcome the thought of countrygoers sharing this countryside.

It is not a particularly easy route to ride for there are several climbs and some equally tricky descents which can be both muddy and slippy after rain. In many respects it is best to wheel your bike over difficult sections. Above all else remember the Mountain Bike code for this bridleway is very popular with walkers and horse riders as well as cyclists. Always give way to others as a matter of goodwill.

Seeing Places

Eastbourne: the seaside resort of Eastbourne grew up in Victorian times to serve the genteel and rich in their pursuit of pleasure. Many of the hotels and the seafront date from this era. The crowning feature must be the ornate iron pier stretching out to sea, the epitome of Victorian ambition.

Jevington: quiet though it may seem now, this huddle of houses has witnessed many a dark deed of smuggling. Some say that the local vicar was also involved in the jaunts organised by the then landlord of the Eight Bells pub, Jack or "Jevington" jig. He was certainly a bit of a lad, for the misdeeds eventually led him to be sentenced to seven years' transportation and later to 14 more at Botany Bay in Australia. The South Downs way passes directly by Jevington Church, a much restored building dating from the last century but this caused a furore at the time as parts of the original building dated from Saxon times.

Alfriston: the Downs hollow to the pretty Cuckmere valley and there stands the equally delicious village of Alfriston which has understandably become something of a honey-pot. The community has done its best to develop tourism without losing its integrity and it is a good place to while away an hour or two or stay overnight. Like Jevington it has an illustrious history of smuggling although the romanticism is somewhat lost when you read of the Alfriston Gang and its murderous deeds. It is all rather tame nowadays. There are antique shops and pubs, and a small museum to greet your arrival.

The Long Man, Wilmington: not seen directly from the route so a minor detour is required. The Long Man is thought to date from the Iron Age possibly being a fertility symbol. Some have suggested that it is an elaborate 19th century folly, but this is an unlikely explanation. The Man is 73 metres in length and carries a staff in each hand, a very impressive sight for miles around.

This is a linear route. The idea is to use the rail service to get back to the starting point at Eastbourne. The trains on this line run hourly and there is currently ample space for bikes.

The Route

1. It seems appropriate that the ride starts from Eastbourne Pier, a well-known meeting place in the town. Turn left to ride along the wide Grand Parade.

2. Turn right into Carlisle Road and continue along this quiet thoroughfare which is truncated firstly by Compton Street and, further up, by the busier Meads Road where care should be taken when making the required left and then right manoeuvres.

3. Cross Galdick Road passing by college buildings. Continue into Paradise Drive which rises towards the downs. After Link Road, look for the start of the South Downs Way on your left heralded by an information board and metal barrier.

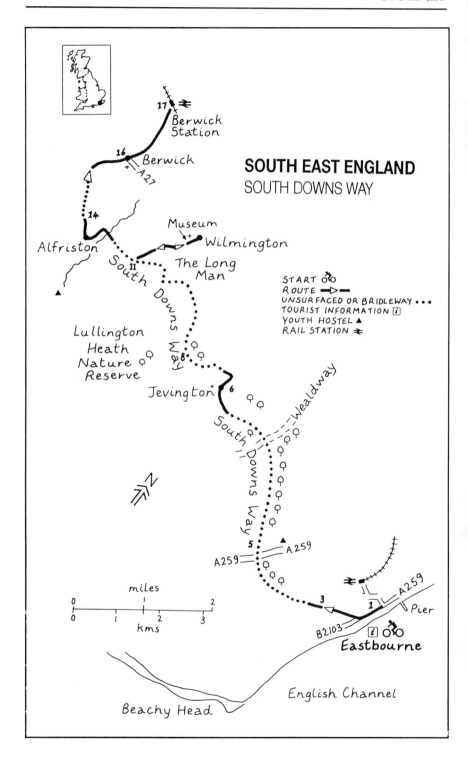

SOUTH EAST ENGLAND
SOUTH DOWNS WAY

START 🚲
ROUTE ➡️━
UNSURFACED OR BRIDLEWAY •••
TOURIST INFORMATION ⓘ
YOUTH HOSTEL ▲
RAIL STATION ⇌

4. The Way is very well waymarked with an acorn symbol and blue bridleway arrow. It is a wide track here climbing up the hillside and curving right to rise more steeply to the top. Keep ahead to the A259, an unpleasant road which should be crossed with a degree of caution.

5. Once over it is plain sailing for miles to Jevington. The track first runs through a golf course then above Eastbourne with good views to the sea. It then curves left to a summit, just past the trig point where it is crossed by the Weald Way. From here it is a downhill run down Bourne Hill.

6. The track enters the village of Jevington by an old pump. At the road junction go right. There's a choice of routes here. For those wishing to see the church, turn left by the enterprising Hungry Monk restaurant. Note the plaque advising that this is the birthplace of Banoffi Pie in 1972, one of the best loved puddings in the world! Follow Church Road to the church and the South Downs Way continues ahead up the hillside which is not any easy ascent.

7. The alternative is not to turn left into Church Lane but to continue through the village to the Eight Bells, a deservedly popular hostelry in these parts (no smuggling these days!). Look for a bridleway on the left about 200 metres beyond, opposite the Old Post Office. Follow this.

8. Ignore the bridleway which leads off to the right and the track which leads straight on. Your way bears left and runs up the bank between bushes and trees. It is tricky in places as a channel has been created to drain the bridleway.

9. Whichever route is chosen they should meet in the woods to become a wider track. You reach a junction, no doubt in need of a breather. Turn right here along a short narrow section to a bridle gate.

10. The way becomes a green swathe across Lullington Heath, high-level bliss away from it all and a joy to ride. It soon becomes a track again, running above the intriguing dry valley of Lullington known as Deep Dean. The Way then drops down to a metalled road where visibility is limited so listen keenly.

11. It would be sacrilegious not to see the Long Man at Wilmington, so go right along this lane until a suitable vantage point is found. You might also wish to continue to the lovely village of Wilmington but whatever your desire return to the Way to regain the route to Alfriston.

12. If not diverting for the Long Man you cross the metalled road mentioned above and the narrow way drops to a house by a junction. Go ahead, as signposted to Alfriston, at the triangular junction. Proceed across the bridge over the River Cuckmere and turn left at the junction.

13. Ride into Alfriston gently, for you deserve a break. In the village square turn right to pass by Ye Olde Smugglers Inn which sports a fine vintage CTC sign. Continue straight on now to leave the village climbing to a crossroads.

14. Go ahead here along a bridleway marked to Firle (4 miles). This is a possible extension for those seeking a few more miles. The aggregate track dips down then approaches a house known as Comp Barn. You continue ahead along a narrow way, bumping over tree routes along what can be a very muddy section after rain.

15. You emerge onto a wider bridleway. Turn right (unless you elect for the extension through to Firle and Glynde where there is a railway station). The way becomes a concrete drive which passes by barns on the left and then curves right to a junction in the sleepy hamlet of Berwick.

16. The road leads by yester-year cottages and the Cricketers Arms, a characterful Harveys pub well worth pulling your brakes on for. You reach the main A27 road, a fast stretch to be crossed but the visibility is good.

17. Once over, a narrow road leads to a junction where you turn left for Berwick Station. Trains return to Eastbourne from the far platform across the level crossing. There is very little to occupy the time here so plan your arrival so as not to be stranded between trains.

Great Cycling Ideas

The main area of interest for off-road cycling tends to be concentrated on the South Downs Way which is the only National Trail which can be cycled from end to end. There are other places though including the Cuckoo Trail (which is much more gentle) which looks set to be extended. There are also plans to develop far more cycle routes than present in Kent; countryside rides between seaside towns and across the rolling North Downs.

London

On Your Bike, LCC's Guide to Cycling in London. The London Cycling Campaign publishes the essential information - a valuable companion. Price about £4.00. "The Green London Way" by Bob Gilbert is also available. Price about £10. Tel: 0171 928 7220 for details.

Richmond Cycle Route Network Map: this map suggests routes through one of London's most famous parks.

Kent

Alkam Valley Rides, Blue Bell Hill Rides and **Wye and Crundale Rides** introduce the cyclist to some of Kent's garden countryside. Small charge for each leaflet.

Cycling Around Canterbury: a series of leaflets outlining rides to local beauty spots, churches and villages out of the busy cathedral city of Canterbury. The rides range from 10-16 miles. Small charge.

Cycling in Kent: a series of leaflets including runs between Pegwell Bay and Birchington and from Canterbury to Sandwich and Folkstone. Tel: East Kent Tourism (01227) 764513.

East Sussex

Cuckoo Trail: railmen on the old railway from Polegate through to Eridge nicknamed this the Cuckoo Line because the first cuckoo of the Spring is said to have been freed at Heathfield Fair every year. The cycle path from Polegate to Heathfield, 12 miles at present, offers an off-road slice of paradise in this locale, although it is truncated in places.

Dyke Railway Trail: a short (two-mile) but enjoyable off-road path from Hangleton near Hove to Devil's Dyke. There are several routes on the downs above Brighton which are popular with cyclists.

Forest Way: a path which runs from East Grinstead to Groombridge for approximately 9 to 10 miles on an old track bed of a branch of the London, Brighton and South Coast Railway. One endearing feature is the numbers of oasts witnessed from the route. Oasts were used throughout the area for drying hops on many local farms. Leaflet available. Small charge.

Old Romney Church, Kent (Shepway District Council)

South Downs Way: 99 miles of National Trail along the South Downs which has become deservedly popular with mountain bikers in pursuit of the elixir of life. The chalk downs offer views across the Sussex Weald and to the Sussex Coast. The route begins at Buriton near Winchester and runs through to Eastbourne. Leaflets and books available.

Sussex Cycle Pack: an excellent presentation of four routes - *The Devil and The Deep Blue Sea, The Cuckoo Trail, 1066 Country* and *The Martyrs, The Saints & The Old White Giant.* As the titles suggest, each route is packed with historical intrigue from Iron Age tribes to William the Conqueror. Ranging from 10 to 25 miles with extensions if needed. Price range: £1 - £2. Tel: East Sussex County Council on (01273) 481000.

West Sussex

Countryside Cycling Pack: Six outings (mainly on roads) including the Chichester Downs, in Rother Valley, and Sussex Weald. They're all good rides. Price range: £2 - £3. Tel: West Sussex County Council on (01243) 777420.

Cycling in and Around Adur: a set of route cards suggesting cycle trips in Adur. Price: about £2.

Cycling Round West Sussex: a route around the county linking Chichester and Arundel via The Bluebell railway, etc. About 200 miles, some on roads. Leaflet available.

Deers Leap Park: Mountain Bike Tracks, Saint Hill Green, East Grinstead. Tel: (01342) 325858 for details.

Worth Way: a six-mile route from Three Bridges station near Crawley to East Grinstead.

Surrey

Downs Link: great route running from Steyning to Guildford, a distance of 30 miles of mainly railway path between the South and North Downs. Leaflet available.

Get Cycling in Surrey: a booklet which highlights eight possible outings in Surrey from the Waverley villages to Leigh and Outwood. Price range: £2 - £3.

Leith Hill Tower, Surrey (Action Packs)

Cycle Holiday Companies

*Bespoke Holidays,*6 Bank Street, Hythe, Kent KT21 5AN. Tel: (01303) 230404. Tailor made holidays.

Best of Britain Cycle Touring, PO Box 9548, London, SW17 0ZJ. Open: all year. Tel: 0181 767 6305.

Garden of England Cycling Holidays, Barn Cottage, Harbourland, Boxley, Maidstone, Kent ME14 3DN. Open: all year. Tel: (01622) 675891.

Cycle Hire Companies

London:

Cyclecare Olympia, 30 Blythe Road, W14 0HA. Open: all year. Tel: 0171 602 9757; *Cyclelogical,* 302 Holloway Road, N7 and 136 New Cavendish Street, W1; Open: all year. Tel: 0171 700 6611; *De Vere Cycles,* 630 Streatham High Road, SW16 3QL. Open: all year. Tel: 0181 679 6197; *Bridge Bikes,* 137 Putney Bridge Road, SW15 2PA. Open: all year (not Sundays). Tel: (0181) 8703934.

Also try The London Bicycle Company at Gabriel's Wharf, SE1 Tel: 0171 928 7220. Tours of London by bike.

Kent:

Ashford: *Short Cut Tours,* PO Box 189, TN23 5ZU. Open: All year. Tel: (01233) 633299. Day rides and holidays.

Bewl Water: *Bewl Water Bike Hire,* Bewl Water, Lamberhurst. Open: May to November. Tel: (01860) 386144.

Deal: *Park Cycles,* Rear of 42 High Street, CT14 6HE. Open: Mid March to October. Tel: (01304) 366080. BR.

Dover: *Andy's Cycles,* 156 London Road. Open: all year. Tel: (01304) 204401. BR.

Dymchurch: *Harrison Cycle Hire,* New Beach Holiday Centre, Hythe Road. Open: Summer only. *The Cycle Shop,* 57 High Street, TN29 0NH. Open: all year but check times. Tel: (01303) 875296.

Folkstone: *Renham's Cycle Centre,* 17 Grace Hill. Open: Summer only. Tel: (01303) 241884. BR.

Margate: *Ken's Bikes,* 26/28 Eaton Road, CT9 1XA. Open: all year. Tel: (01843) 221422. BR.

Sevenoaks: *Sevenoaks Cycles,* 41 Dartford Road, Vine Parade. Open: all year. Tel: (01732) 742674. BR.

Surrey:

Camberley: *Wellington Trek,* 24, Wellington Road, GU17 8AN. Open: all year. Tel: (01344) 772797.

Cranleigh: *Motosport,* GU6 8JJ. Open: all year, exceptt Mondays Tel: (01483) 278282.

East Horsley: *Horsley Cycles,* Station Approach. Open: Summer only. Tel: (01483) 284298. BR.

Haslemere: *D.S. Cycles,* 105 Wey Hill, Haslemere, GU27 1HS. Open: all year. Tel: (01428) 656885. BR.

Horsham: *A & D Cycles,* 31 Queen Street, RH13 5HA. Open: all year. Tel: (01403) 258391. *Southwater Cycles,* Unit 6, Southwater Industrial Estate, Station Rd, RH13 7UD. Tel: (01403) 732561. BR.

Westhumble: *Action Packs,* Westhumble Station (Box Hill) near Dorking. Tel: (01306) 886944. BR.

East Sussex:

Brighton: *Sunrise Cycle Hire,* West Pier Promenade, Kings Road. Open: Summer Only. Tel: (01273) 748881. BR.

Forest Row: *Future Cycles,*Friends Yard, London Road, RH18 5EE. Open: all year. Recumbents available, holidays can also be arranged.

Hastings: *Hastings Cycle Hire and Sales,* Above St Andrew's Square Market, South Terrace, Hastings, TN34 1SJ. Open: all year. Tel: (01424) 444013. BR.

Rye: *Surf Shack,* Market Road, TN31 7JA. Open: all year. Tel: (01797) 225746. BR.

Seven Sisters Country Park: (near Alfriston) *Forest Cycle Hire,* Granary Barn, Seven Sisters Country Park, Exceat, BN25 4AD. Open: all year. Tel: (01323) 870310. Holidays can be arranged. A cycling centre for disabled people is being established here.

Opposite: Bike on hire from Future Cycles! (Frank Spooner)

West Sussex:

Chichester: *2XS Mountain Bike Hire,* Bookwood Road, West Wittering, near Chichester PO20 8LT. Open: all year. Tel: (01243) 512552.

Horsham: *Southwater Cycles,* Station Road, RH13 7LD. Open: all year except Tuesdays. Tel: (01403) 732561.

Stop Press: Try also *Orchard Trails,* 5 Orchard Way, Horsmonden, Tonbridge. Cycle Holidays Tel: (01892) 722680.

HEART OF ENGLAND

Includes Gloucestershire, Hereford & Worcester, Shropshire, Staffordshire, Warwickshire, West Midlands.
Tourist Information: Heart of England Tourist Board, Woodside, Larkhill Road, Worcester, WR5 2EF.
Tel: (01905) 763436

From the literary home of Shakespeare to the turbulent Marches of old, and stretching down from the southern reaches of the Peak District to the Forest of Dean, the Heart of England is packed with cycling opportunities. The Marches, a rich borderland where England meets Wales, rejoices in its half timbered villages and poetic landscapes. Housman's words echo to this day. It is the quietest place under the sun and it is easy enough to get off the beaten track in Shropshire and Herefordshire.

But Gloucestershire is fast becoming a place to be. Not only are there great off-road routes through the Forest of Dean but ample scope to ride into the Cotswolds to yellow stone villages, the grand wool churches and historic houses. Warwickshire has a charm provided not only by the elegant spa town of Leamington and majestic Warwick Castle but also its many tucked away villages to discover; villages such as Charlcote, Tanworth in Arden, Napton on the Hill or Southam. Warwickshire borders into North Worcestershire where there are equally delightful pockets of countryside between Droitwich spa and Redditch. Further south lies the fruit growing area of the Vale of Evesham where the early blossom makes springtime rides all the more pleasant. These are complemented by several superb rides to the north and west of the malvern Hills through the Teme Valley and Wyre Forest, quiet corners which are but an hour from the West Midlands.

The same could be said of Staffordshire where the cyclist can find tranquillity itself in the serene Sow valley, heading for Market Drayton by way of the old coaching town of Eccleshall. Those who seek out more exhilerating routes will turn to the Staffordshire Moorlands or to the permitted routes on Cannock Chase, heathland and forest where fallow and red deer roam.

COUNTRYSIDE RIDE

The Historic Marches

A borderland adventure described by Kay and Chris Dartnell of Wheely Wonderful Cycling

Distance: 46 miles.

Terrain: Moderately easy with a few climbs.

Map: O.S. Landranger 137 Ludlow and Wenlock Edge area.

Rail Access: Ludlow - Wheely Wonderful Cycling can arrange to deliver bikes to Ludlow railway station.

Accommodation and Refreshment: there is ample bed and breakfast or inn accommodation in Ludlow and the villages *en route* including youth hostels and campsites at Ludlow and Clun. There are numerous pubs in the villages. Tourist Information Tel (01584) 875053.

Cycle Hire and Holidays: phone *Wheely Wonderful Cycling* on (01568) 770755

The Ride

"In the valleys of springs of rivers,
By Ony and Teme and Clun,
The country for easy livers,
The quietest under the sun... ".

The words of poet A.E. Housman aptly describe this marvellous route through the Marches, the borderlands of England and Wales where winding lanes offer some of the best cycling in Europe. You'll ride near the sparkling waters of the infant Clun, Redlake and Teme, crossing bridges to Herefordshire and Shropshire villages where half-timbered houses stand and tradition still holds.

The route also takes you by the ruins of five castles, home to Norman overlords who made their mark on the medieval map. It was not without resistance from the Welsh and border peoples attempting to resist the tide of overbearing power. Most of the cycling on the route is

67

easy with a few climbs but, for the most part, the way follows river valleys. Our recommendation is: take your time and enjoy the run over two days. This is, after all, a land for easy livers.

Getting the bike ready for hire at Wheely Wonderful Cycling
(Chris Rushton)

Seeing Places

Ludlow: is often described as an architectural gem with many half-timbered Tudor and fine red brick Georgian town houses lying within the confines of a Norman planned town. The castle, museums and local festivals make it a place to saunter awhile. Ludlow grew rich through the wool trade and while is still very much an agricultural town there is a growing interest in tourism.

Mortimer Forest: named after the powerful Mortimer family, it was once their favourite hunting ground. It is now managed by the Forestry Commission and, in the early part of the day, deer can be seen roaming between the trees.

Wigmore: was an important town in medieval times known to William the Conqueror and to nobility for, over the centuries, the Mortimers had a hand in the affairs of state, sometimes with disastrous effect. Roger de Mortimer was hanged for usurping Edward III's authority despite lavishly banqueting him and his mother, Queen Isabella! The ancient church and castle ruins can be seen at most times. There's a potter and furniture and musical instrument makers in the village who welcome visitors.

Brampton Bryan: must be one of the prettiest villages for miles around with a very nice tea shop and another castle ruin, featured in the film "Howard's End" starring Emma Thompson. It is difficult to see the ruins over the tall hedge. This is the scene of a great siege by Royalists during the English Civil War. The castle was held by Lady Brilliana Harley on behalf of her Parliamentarian husband (who was safe in Oxford at the time).

Clun: is a small farming community where the romantic ruins of Clun castle can be seen nearby, built in the last years of the 11th century by Picot de Say. It suffered many a skirmish including a ransacking by Prince Llewelyn in 1214 and by the famous Welsh warrior, Owain Glyndwr in 1400.

Hopton Castle: is always a surprise when you ride by it. Unlike Clun and Wigmore, Hopton looks far more complete. It is in private grounds so access is not possible. You can, however, see the stream into which bodies were thrown during the English Civil War siege here - a gory affair. Nearby is the Forestry Commission's Hopton Mountain Bike Trail but make sure that you have the energy to detour as there are steep climbs on the circuit.

Leintwardine: was a Roman garrison town (Bravonium) situated on Watling Street West between Caerleon and Chester. It is said that there are extensive remains under the current garage. Nearby Burrington, on the return leg to Ludlow, is famous for its 17th century grave covers which are cast iron, a relic of when the great forge at Bringewood was working.

The Route:

1. Begin at Ludlow Railway station (although car drivers might well start at Elton if hiring from *Wheely Wonderful*). Turn right and then left at a T-junction into Corve Street. Ride up this thoroughfare to pass the half-timbered Feathers Hotel on the left and bear next right at the top heading towards the centre of town (castle and tourist information).

2. Turn left down Broad Street to roll through the only remaining town

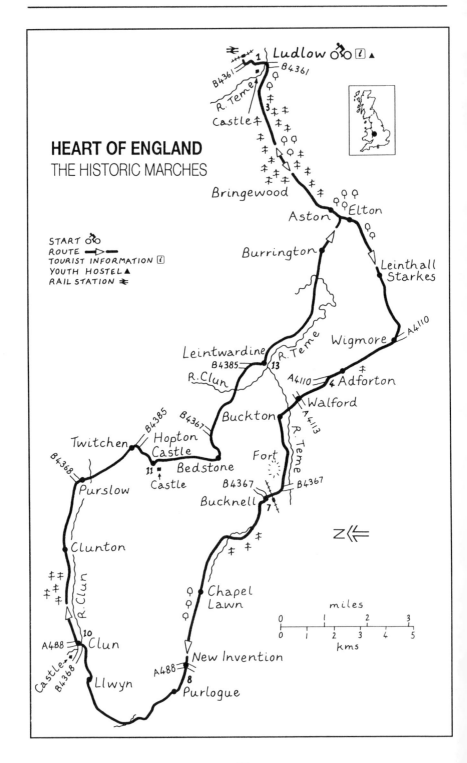

HEART OF ENGLAND
THE HISTORIC MARCHES

Ludlow

B4361

B4361

R. Teme

Castle

Bringewood

Aston

Elton

Burrington

Leinthall
Starkes

Wigmore

A4110

Leintwardine

B4385

R. Teme

13

R. Clun

A4110

Adforton

Walford

Buckton

A4113

R. Teme

B4385

B4367

Twitchen

Hopton
Castle

Fort

B4368

Bedstone

Castle

B4367

B4367

Purslow

Bucknell

Clunton

Chapel
Lawn

R. Clun

New Invention

Clun

A4488

Purlogue

A4488

Castle

B4368

Llwyn

START
ROUTE
TOURIST INFORMATION
YOUTH HOSTEL
RAIL STATION

miles

0   1   2   3

0   1   2   3   4   5

kms

gate. Cross Ludford Bridge and take the first right, opposite Ludlow Youth Hostel, signposted to Wigmore. A steep haul leads you up into Whitcliffe Common with excellent views back over to Ludlow. The road climbs for 2 miles through Mortimer Forest.

3. You are rewarded by a two-mile descent into the Teme Valley. Continue on this road through the hamlets of Pipe Aston, Elton and Leinthall Starkes until you reach Wigmore. At the main A4110 road turn right (signposted Leintwardine). This takes you to Adforton, another village built on a natural gap in higher ground.

4. A quarter of a mile beyond turn left onto the B4350 road (signposted A4113 to Knighton) to the estate village of Walford. Go straight over at the crossroads, signposted to Buckton and Adleymoor. This tiny little lane leads into the water-meadows of the Teme and for the first time since leaving Ludlow that you bridge the river. Look for the kingfishers and dippers.

5. Enter the hamlet of Buckton where there is a mill on the left and you can see the remains of the driving wheel. Immediately after this bear sharp left, continuing on the same road. There are brilliant views of the Teme all along this road.

6. Just past the Adleymoor turn off, take the right-hand fork towards Bucknell, passing Coxall Knoll. The left-hand turn takes you the short distance to Brampton Bryan and is worth the detour. If so retrace your tracks and at the B4367 turn right for Bucknell. Cycle past the sawmill and village sweet-shop, then cross the tracks of the Heart of Wales railway line. The railway station has a cycle rack near to the former impressive station house. If you intend to catch the train you have to wave it down and bike space is limited. Bucknell is an unspoilt village which has managed to retain most of its amenities, including two good public houses which offer refreshment.

7. Once across the level crossing turn left onto the Chapel Lawn road. This runs through Bucknell village and into the valley of the River Redlake. You ride gently upstream, so to speak, as the hills rise around you. Continue through the hamlet of Chapel Lawn to New Invention where you cross the A488.

8. Ride up to the few houses at Purlogue. After one mile turn left at Curlew Corner, just before the bridge across the Redlake. This is a fairly steep but short section, so do not hesitate to pause at any time! At the top of the hill turn right. The undulating road leads through wood and semi-heathland until a final uphill stretch reaches the summit at a crossroads.

9. Go straight on and brace yourself for an exhilarating two-mile run

into Clun by way of Llwyn. There are good views of Clun castle and settlement during the final descent to the top of the village, opposite the church. Turn left and downhill to cross the historic packhorse bridge and the Clun Bridge Tearooms for a well earned break. Clun is the recommended overnight stop.

10. At the T-junction turn right on the B4368 to pass the Sun Inn on the road to Craven Arms. Continue through Clunton and turn right at Purslow by the Hundred House Inn on the road signposted to Leintwardine (B4385). After 1.5 miles turn right to Hopton Castle.

11. Turn left at Hopton Castle (with the castle in front of you), then take the first right to Bedstone (another estate village) and home of Bedstone College public school. Turn left at the T-junction, signposted to Hopton Heath and Craven Arms.

12. After half a mile you go over the railway line, then take the first right to Jay. After the downhill ride, fork left at "The Jay" (name plate is on the gate) to the bridge over the River Clun, passing through meadows and beneath pollarded willows. After the bridge the road rises steeply through a tunnel of trees before opening out again to the first houses of Leintwardine. Turn right at the T-junction onto the main road.

13. At the Lion Hotel, before the bridge over the Teme, go left to ride through the village past the Fiddlers Tearoom and onwards on the road signposted to Downton through the Teme Valley. Ignore the left turning to Downton but continue on the road to Burrington and, at the T-junction at Elton, turn left for Ludlow. It may be a climb back up through Mortimer's Forest but the last downhill section brings a perfect end to a glorious Marches cycle ride.

GREAT CYCLING IDEAS!

The Heart of England has much to offer, for the cycle tourer especially. There are, however, increasing opportunities for the off-road cyclist especially in the Forest of Dean, and other locations such as Hopton Castle in Shropshire. Gloucestershire has become a much improved place for the recreational cyclist but Hereford & Worcester and Shropshire are looking to build on their current base to attract more cyclists in the future.

Gloucestershire

Cycle Routes in Cheltenham/Gloucester: Designed for town cycling.

Cycle Touring Routes in Gloucestershire: a set of exceptionally good routes devised by Gloucestershire County Council. Price: about £2. Tel: Gloucestrershire County Council, (01452) 425673.

Nailsworth to Stonehouse linear route: a 5.5 mile off-road way in the Stroud valley, which is very attractive.

Cycling in the Forest of Dean: Excellent introduction to family cycling through the Forest. Leaflets available. There are several routes in preparation by the Railways to Cycleways Project.

Cotswold Water Park Cycle Routes: leaflet available explaining routes around the Park.

The Inside Track to Mountain Biking in the Cotswolds: Excellent pack available from the Cotswold Cycling Company. Tel: (01242) 250642.

Hereford and Worcester

Cycling in Herefordshire: a leaflet highlighting routes in Herefordshire's rich pastures including the Black and White villages.

Cycle Route Guide to Hereford and Worcester: 10 routes and a main circular route. These routes provide a good introduction to this part of the Marches. Available in a pack. Price range: £1 - £2.

Cycle Route Guide around North East Worcestershire: leaflet available describing routes around the quieter roads of North East Worcestershire.

Easy Cycle Routes from Ross-on-Wye: leaflet about gentle circular rides ideal for families. Small charge.

Shropshire

Bike-It in Telford: a very useful map illustrating cycle ways and routes in Ironbridge and Telford. Also a series of cycle rides in leaflet form.

Corvedale Cycle Tour: a 40-mile tour through several lovely Shropshire villages in Corvedale. Leaflet available. Small charge.

Cycling For Pleasure in The Marches: superb cycle routes mapped out in Shropshire and Leominster district. Easy graded routes and little traffic. Researched by the Wheely Wonderful team and published by Shropshire Books.

Exploring Shropshire, Countryside & Woodland Cycle Trails: booklet. Price: about £1.

Hopton Mountain Bike Trail: a leaflet describing a mountain bike route opened by Forest Enterprise in the western hills of the county near to Hopton Castle.

Jack Mytton Way: a 72-mile route from Billingsley and Llanfair Water-dine which traverses much of the county. The route is shared with others so it can get exceedingly muddy and is quite a challenge for off-road cyclists.

Silkin Way: a town way from Bratton and Coalport which provides access to Coalbrookdale and Iron Bridge, a World Heritage Site. 14 miles. Leaflet available.

Staffordshire

Biddulph Valley Way: from Biddulph to Congleton along an old rail track, approximately 5 miles. You can ride off to Biddulph Grange gardens and Country Park.

Cannock Chase: popular for mountain biking - stay on the bridleways please. One of England's great old forests.

Churnet Valley: cycling through the Churnet Valley is gorgeous and there is an off-road section on the old railway track between Alton and Denstone - about 4 miles.

Cycle and See the Staffordshire Moorlands: six brilliant routes throughout the Staffordshire Moorlands. Try the Cycling and Poetry ride. Price: about £2-3. Tel: (01538) 381000.

Cycle Rides in & around Lichfield District: a booklet describing fourteen rides from 6-48 miles, by Lichfield District Council. Price 50p.

Freewheelers: leaflets outlining simple routes within Lichfield District.

Kingswinford Branch Railway Walk: runs south of Wolverhampton for 8 miles along the old Great Western branch line. Stop for tea at Wombourne.

Summer cycling at Wetton Mill (Chris Rushton)

Manifold Trail: a route par excellance on the track-bed of the Manifold Valley Light Railway. Passes by Thor's Cave and Wetton Mill. Exceptional scenery. On Sundays, the place is taken over by cycles.

Rudyard Lake: the old North Staffordshire railway track-bed offers 9 miles off-road from Rushton to Leek, running alongside the tranquil waters of Rudyard Lake.

Stafford to Newport Greenway: another old track-bed offering a traffic free route out of Stafford to Gnosall and the Shropshire Union Canal. Not quite reached Newport yet.

Warwickshire

The Greenway: a 2.5-mile railway path south of Stratford through Shakespeare's country. Pleasant surprise.

West Midlands

Birmingham and Black Country Canal Cycleway: 14 miles of cycling along towpaths between Birmingham and Wolverhampton which offers a marvellous traffic free route.

Cycle Rides Around Birmingham: leaflets from Pushbikes. Small charge for each leaflet.

West Midlands Bicycle Rides: Price range £3 - £4. Published by the Birmingham Cycling Project.

Cycle Holiday Companies

Acorn Activities, 7 East Street, Hereford HR1 4RY. Open: all year. Tel: (01432) 357335. Offers cycling breaks in The Marches and Wales. BR.

Cycle Easy, Rays Farm, Billingsley, Bridgnorth, WV16 6PF. Open: Holidays from Easter to September but cycle hire is available all year. Excellent base for Jack Mytton Way. Tel: (01299) 841255.

Cotswold Cycling Company, 48 Shurdington Road, Cheltenham Spa, Gloucestershire, GL53 OJE. Open: all year. Tel: (01242) 250642. Cycle Hire also available. BR.

Intrepid Cycle Tours, Manor Farm, Napton, Rugby, Warks CV23 8NF. Open: April to Sept. Cycle hire available all year. Tel: (01926) 815418.

Pedal for Pleasure - Cotswold Cycling Holidays, 45 Bisley Old Road, Stroud, Gloucestershire GL5 1LU. Open: March to October. Tel: (01453) 762233.

Pedalaway, Trereece Barn, Llangarron, HR9 6NH. Open: all year. Tel: (01989) 770357.

Spokes Cycle Tours - see listing in West Country. Tel: (01454) 238199.

Steel-away, The Butts, Poulton, Circencester, GL7 5HY. Tel: (01285) 851356. 90% off-road tours.

Year 2000 International, 5 Sandstar Close, Longlevens, GL2 ONR. Open: all year. Tel: (01452) 501361. Mountain bike coaching. CH available all year. BR.

Wheely Wonderful Cycling, Petchfield Farm, Elton, Nr Ludlow, SY8 2HJ. Open: all year. Tel: (01568) 770755. A welcoming company offering self-guided tours in Shropshire and the Welsh borderland. CH available.

Cycle Hire Companies

Gloucestershire:

Cannop, Forest of Dean: *Pedalabikeaway*, Cannop Valley, Near Coleford, GL16 7EH. Open: excellent centre open most days. Tel: (01594) 860065.

Cheltenham: *Crabtrees*, 50 Winchcombe Street, GL52 2ND. Open: April to October. Tel: (01242) 515291. BR.

Moreton-in-Marsh: *B. Jeffrey*, The Toy Shop, High Street, GL56 0AD. Open: Mon. to Sat. half-day Wed. Tel: (01608) 650756.

Stroud: *Severnvale Specialist Bikes*, Unit 3, Fromeside Industrial Park, Dr Newtons Way, GL5 3JA. Open: all year. Tel: (01453) 755034. BR.

Wootton Under Edge: *Tangent*, 22-24 Bradley Street, GL12 7AR. Open: all year. Tel: (01453) 844750.

Hereford and Worcester:

Evesham: *Jack Honeybourne Cycles*, 7 Vine Mews, WR11 4RE. Open: all year. Tel: (01386) 41867. BR.

Hereford: *Coombes Cycles*, 94 Widemarsh Street HR4 9HG. Open: all year. Tel: (01432) 354373. BR.

Kington: *Offa's Bikes,* Church House, Church Road, Kington, HR5 3AG. Tel: (01544) 230534. Accommodation too.

Leominster: *Slim Willy's,* High St. Open: all year. Tel: (01568) 614052. BR.

Munsley: *Munsley Acre Country Guesthouse,* near Ledbury, HR8 2SH. Open: all year. Tel: (01531) 670568. Accommodation available and itineraries supplied.

Ross-on-Wye: *Revolutions,* Little and Hall, Broad Street, NR9 7DY. Open: all year. Tel: (01989) 562639.

Shropshire:

Church Stretton: *Longmynd Cycles,* Sandford Court, Sandford Avenue, SY6 6BH. Open: all year. Tel: (01694) 722367. BR.

Ludlow: *Pearce Engineering,* Fishmore, SY8 3DP. Open: all year but Sundays by arrangement. Tel: (01584) 876016.

Oswestry: *Stuart Barkley Cycles,* Salop Road, SY11 2NU. Open: all year. Tel: (01691) 658705; *Karhire,* Bridge Service Station, Gobowen Road. Open: all year. Tel (01691) 653520.

Shrewsbury: *Dave Mellor Cycles,* 20 Frankwell, SY3 8JY. Open: Mon-Sat all year by arrangement only. Tel: (01743) 366662.

Staffordshire:

Lichfield: *Graham's Cycles,* 10 Wheel Lane, WS13 7EA. Open: all year. Tel: (01543) 257906. BR.

Stoke-on-Trent: *Roy Swinnerton,* 67-73 Victoria Road, Fenton, ST4 2HG. Open: all year. Tel: (01782) 747782. BR.

Waterhouses: *Brown End Farm Cycle Hire,* ST10 3JR. Open: Easter to September but according to demand during the remainder of the year. Tel: (01538) 308313; *Waterhouses Cycle Hire,* Old Station Car Park, ST10 3EG. Open: April to September. Tel: (01538) 308609.

Warwickshire:

Stratford-upon-Avon: *Clarkes Stratford Cycle Shop,* Bancroft Esso Station, Guild Street, CU37 6QZ. Open: all year. Tel: (01789) 205057.

EAST ANGLIA

Includes Bedfordshire, Cambridgeshire, Essex,
Hertfordshire, Norfolk, Suffolk.
Tourist Information: East Anglia Tourist Board,
Topplesfield Hall, Hadleigh, Suffolk IP7 5DN. Tel: (01743)
822922

There's more than a touch of old England in East Anglia and the sense
of isolation in Norfolk and Suffolk becomes apparent when cycling along
forgotten lanes which lead to flint villages. Bedfordshire, Hertfordshire
and Essex are more populated but they still offer great rides from
historic towns such as Bedford, home to John Bunyan, the author of
A Pilgrim's Progress or Hadleigh in Essex, where the romantic castle
ruins inspired one of John Constable's famous paintings.

One of the loveliest rides is through Constable Country on the borders
of Essex and Suffolk to the timbered houses of Lavenham and Kersey or
Flatford Mill, an area of gently undulating fields, corn swaying in the
breeze. But Suffolk offers miles of quiet routes which pass by old mills,
historic houses and to Victorian seaside resorts such as Southwold.

Norfolk, too, is an excellent destination for the cyclist with coastal
rides between such resorts as Great Yarmouth and Cromer or through
the wild heathland of Breckland to the market town of Dereham.

Cambridge, with its old colleges and winding streets, makes an
excellent but busy base for touring the fens and perhaps riding through
to the cathedral city of Ely or onward to Wisbech on the Wash. From
Kings Lynn, there are several pleasant runs through lavender fields to
the Royal Estate at Sandringham and to the market town of Fakenham.

Whichever area you choose you will find superb cycling in East
Anglia as for the most part it is gently undulating and not flat (its all
relative)! Nevertheless, it is no place for those who thrive on harder
climbs. The cathedral city of Norwich is the main centre and is probably
your starting point for a tour of The Broads, the UK's newest National
Park which covers a unique landscape of water and wetland where the
lanes wind through grazing pastures and by reed-fringed channels.

COUNTRYSIDE RIDE

The Lost Capital of East Anglia

Distance: 80 miles.

Terrain: Easy going two-day ride.

Map: O.S. Landranger 156 Saxmundham, Aldeburgh and surrounding area.

Rail Access: Saxmundham, Darsham (for Byways Cycle Hire) or Halesworth.

Accommodation and Refreshment: there are several public houses on the route and tea rooms in Walberswick, Southwold, Halesworth and Framlington. Accommodation is also available throughout. Contact Aldeburgh Tourist Information on (01728) 453637 or Southwold Tourist Information on (01502) 724729.

Cycle Hire: *Byways Cycle Hire at Darsham.* Tel: (01728) 668764.

The Ride

The back roads of Suffolk are fine for cycling. They are quiet and gently undulating, making for ideal cycling. Ride to the seashore of the North Sea, which retains a romantic Dickensian appeal. The omnipresence of Sizewell on the horizon is a less-pleasing reminder of the 20th century, but even this can be momentarily swept from the mind as you cycle east to the lost capital of East Anglia, beneath the sands of Dunwich.

Seeing Places

Saxmundham: the small town of Saxmundham is a compact, sleepy little town nestled around the market hall. It makes a good starting point for the Suffolk adventure as it is something of a transport interchange between trains and buses.

Minsmere: the RSPB nature reserve welcomes cyclists who leave their bikes at the visitor centre and explore the reserve on foot; it is an extensive reserve in woodland and marsh.

Dunwich: 'Lost Capital' - some might scorn, but kings were crowned here and it was decidedly a cathedral city until the latter part of the 9th century. In medieval times it was a port of considerable repute, receiving a charter from King John in the last year of the 12th century. But the sea reigns supreme on this coast and through the centuries the capital has been lost to the waters. In 1904, the ancient church of All Saints finally crumbled beneath the waves and some say you can hear the bells tolling at low tide. A fitting epitaph for a city no more.

Cyclo-camping in North Norfolk (North Norfolk District Council)

Walberswick: in many respects, the loss of Dunwich became the fortune of Walberswick. After the reconstruction of the Blyth Channel to the sea, there came an erratic but sometimes flourishing trade to the village, especially fishing. The village green has many picturesque houses, a store and café and a local wine shop.

Southwold: this has to be a fine example of a Victorian seaside resort with its wide greens, promenade walks and pebble beach complete with traditional shops, hotels and its very own independent brewery. It makes an ideal overnight stop for the ride. There is a good local museum in addition to the Lifeboat Museum and, as to be expected, there's also a Sailors' Reading Room to catch up on nautical matters.

Halesworth: the main shopping street is pedestrianised but makes a very pleasant sojourn from the ride. There is a small museum and art gallery in the town too.

Framlington: the glory of the town is the castle, a formidable structure which has done well through the centuries to survive so intact given that Mary I's supporters gathered here for battle and, in Elizabeth I's reign, unruly priests were incarcerated here.

There are also, of course, the vineyards of the valleys which are mentioned in the route instructions.

Preparing for hire at Byways Bicycle Centre (Les Lumsdon)

The Route

1. Begin at Saxmundham railway station which also houses a café. Ride down Station Road, past the Bell Hotel, then turn left into High Street.

2. Leave town in the direction of Kelsale but look for a right-hand turn signposted to Theberton. Ignore turnings to the right and left until you reach Theberton Woods. Do not take the first right at the woods but follow the main route right at the next junction.

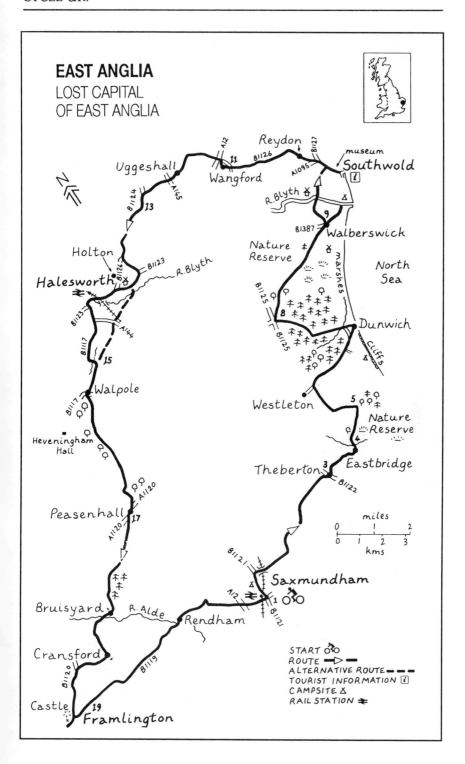

EAST ANGLIA
LOST CAPITAL
OF EAST ANGLIA

3. Turn right onto the B1122 in the village, climb the bank and turn first left by the thatched parish church. This delightful narrow lane leads to Eastbridge, where a left turn is made followed by two more in succession. Do not be hasty at the latter for, on the right is the Eel's Foot, one of Suffolk's many characterful pubs and you'll pass more than a dozen on this expedition. Look at the pub sign here, for you'll not find another quite like it in the land.

4. The road crosses over the Minsmere River, a narrow channel at most times but surrounded by water meadows and reed beds. The road bends right for Minsmere RSPB nature reserve. This has road bumps at regular intervals to keep speeds down.

5. At the junction before the farm keep ahead if you wish to call in to the visitor centre and shop. Otherwise go left and in half a mile turn right as signposted to Dunwich. At the next-junction turn right for Dunwich, a sea breeze rippling against your face as you ride through Westleton Heath. You might also see a right hand turn for Dunwich Heath, over 200 acres of sandy cliffs and a mile of beach. You could make a detour here to take a break at the Coastguard Cottages where there is also an exhibition.

6. Otherwise, keep ahead as the road leads into Dunwich where you turn right to the beach. Pass by the ruins of Greyfriars Abbey and, at the corner by the Ship Inn, keep ahead for the beach car park.

7. Back to the Ship and a few doors along is the fascinating little museum which partly unfolds the mystery of Dunwich. This road runs through Dunwich Forest to join the B1125 road.

8. There is a little by-way on the right through Walberswick nature reserve. This is a sandy track easily traversed by ATBs and hybrids but those on tourers should ride it with care. It becomes a metalled road at Westwood Lodge. Turn right at its end for Walberswick Ferry.

9. Those not using the ferry should turn left instead and right down Palmers Lane. Follow this narrow road, the route of the Southwold light railway, across Walberswick Common to a bridge over the Blyth. Pedal a little further and dismount to walk your bike a quarter of a mile through a golf course to Southwold. Alternatively you can continue along the old railway route to the main road and turn right.

10. Turn left into York road and next right for the town centre, the greens and the sea. Otherwise, go left at the main road (A1095), Station Road, to leave this Victorian haunt behind. Cross Buss Creek to Reydon, where you turn second right onto the B1125 to Wangford, passing Reydon church and Reydon Hall beyond.

11. The road approaches Wangford and turns right. Keep ahead along Church Street and right again into the High Street of this handsome village. Turn left onto the B road again and be very wary at the next junction. Your route is ahead at this most awkward staggered junction. Traffic speeds quickly along here, so be vigilant - especially if there are children with you. Bear slightly right across the westbound carriageways to join the right-hand refuge with a road arrow pointing right. Then look left before crossing the eastbound carriageways.

12. The road beyond runs peacefully through fields where pigs muck about free range style. You come to a junction by Church Farm where you turn left. Turn left in the hamlet of Uggeshall and right and left at the main A145.

13. Ride through to the B1124. Turn left and follow this for 2 miles if going into the town of Halesworth. Those seeking a detour should look for Primes Lane on the left, after passing a factory in Holton. Join the B1123 where you turn right and then first left for Mells.

14. This road dips down through rich water-meadows to the hamlet of Mells. Keep ahead at the T-junction, signposted to Walpole. Go over the level crossing and the main A144 road. The lane passes by the elegant Westhaston Grange and further along by the curious cockpit of a fighter plane seemingly in someone's garden.

15. Join the B1117 and climb towards Walpole. After the church the road dips and you turn left to Sibton and Peasenhall. This is probably the hardest section of the route with a continuous climb to Threadbare Farm and a water tower at the summit.

16. Just beyond is a crossroads and a cut-off left for Darsham. Otherwise descend to Shibdon, bearing right at the White Horse public house. Go next right and right again at the main A1120 road at Peasenhall.

17. Turn left immediately after the church to pass by cottages and farms on back lanes to Bruisyard. Keep ahead at the first junction and turn right at Wood Farm. The road soon joins another but keep left along the edge of Bruisyard Wood. Follow this route through to Bruisyard Church and beyond is the vineyard.

18. Once over the infant Alde, turn right and first left to Cransford. Go right here for just under a mile to the B1120 road. Turn left for Framlingham passing by the Shawgate vineyard.

19. Having visited Framlingham, leave town on the B1119 (passed on the way in) for the final section, a good 7-mile ride to Saxmundham but take care as you cross the Saxmundham by pass.

Great Cycling Ideas

This is definitely cycling country, and the deeper into East Anglia you travel, the better it gets. There are absolutely miles of quiet country lanes in Cambridgeshire, Suffolk and Norfolk which provide very rewarding cycling especially those routes which pass attractions or divert into the villages of East Anglia.

Bedfordshire

Bedfordshire Cycle Routes: a series of cycle routes which enable the cyclist to explore the nooks and crannies of the county. Leaflet available.

Icknield Way Path Riders Route: this way covers 95 miles from Gatley Hill in Bedfordshire to Bridgham Heath in Norfolk. Much of it is open to cyclists but the tracks can be very variable.

Cambridgeshire

Cycle Routes in Cambridge: routes which show how to get about the city with the minimum of hassle. Leaflet available.

Cycling in The Fens, in The Cambridge Green Belt, and also in the Ouse Valley: very attractively-produced packs available suggesting tours into the fens including a lovely run through to Ely. Price: about £2.

Grafham Water: a series of tracks around this large reservoir with excellent cycle hire facilities. Leaflet available.

The Fens: a guide packed with information. Free.

There and Back Again: Cycle rides around Cambridge.

Essex

Country Rides: a series of country rides around Bardfield, Basildon, Belchamps, Epping, Pleshley, Takeley. Designed primarily for horse-riders but for cyclists too.

Flitch Way: Braintree Railway Station to Hatfield Forest, 14 miles. A shared route which can be difficult in places.

Mark Hall Cycle Museum: Muskham Road, Harlow, Essex. Tel: (01279) 439680.

Three Cycle Tours Around Braintree District: leaflet available which illustrates three delightful routes in the Braintree area, a much underrated part of the world.

Uttlesford - A Cyclist's Guide: leaflet available for this little-known but beautiful area.

Hertfordshire

Alban Way: a basic link between St Albans and Hatfield, 6.5 miles.

Cycling in the Hertfordshire Countryside: a series of rides each starting and ending in one of the larger towns of East Hertfordshire. Leaflet.

Nicky Line: off-road link between Harpenden and Hemel Hempstead, 6 miles.

Town and Country Cycle Rides from Stevenage Series, No 1 to Whitwell: a 13 mile ride. Leaflet.

Norfolk

Breckland by Bicycle: leaflet describing several road routes in this attractive part of Norfolk. A good area on which to base a short break.

Marriott's Way: a 21-mile way between Hellesdon and Attlebridge and Aylsham now open to cyclists.

Norfolk Cycleway: fold-out map and route guide available. Small charge. Tel: Norfolk County Council on (01603) 222718.

Peddar's Way: a 50-mile route designed mainly for horse riders but available for cyclists between Bridgham Heath and Holme-next-the-Sea.

Seven Cycle Routes in North Norfolk: a selection of good off-the-beaten-track routes for the cyclist. Small charge.

Weaver's Way: Aylsham to Stalham - 9 miles section open to cyclists. Can get in a muddy state.

Suffolk

Alton Water: a series of cycle tracks around this water park. Cycle hire.

Cycling in Thetford Forest Park: a leaflet illustrating off-road routes through the forest. Nearby is Center Parcs where guests are encouraged to leave the car behind and see the forest by bike.

Godric Way: a 24-mile route based on Bungay. Leaflet available.

Stanton Country Rides: 18 miles of suggested routes. Leaflet to buy.

Suffolk Cycleway: 225 miles of quiet back routes through Suffolk. Also Suffolk Heritage Coast Route.

Three Forests Cycle Trail: a run through back lanes and off-road forest tracks in East Suffolk. Small charge for booklet.

Cycle Holiday Companies

Anglia Cycling Holidays, Ballintuim Post Office, Nr Blairgowrie, Perthshire, Scotland PH10 7NJ. Open: all year. Tel: (01250) 886201. Self-guided holidays throughout East Anglia.

Bicycle Breaks, 71 High St, Colchester., CO1 1UE. Open: All year. Tel: (01206) 868254. Themed bicycle tours.

Green Wheels Cycling Holidays, Aylmerton Field Study Centre, Aylmerton, Norwich, NR11 8RA. Open: all year. Tel: (01263) 837759.

Just Pedalling, 9 Church St, Coltishall, Norfolk N12 7DW. Open: all year. Tel: (01603) 737201. Self-guided tours arranged. Cycle hire available.

Norfolk Cycling Holidays, Sandy Way, Ingoldisthorpe, Kings Lynn, PE31 6NJ. Open: all year. Tel: (01485) 540642. A variety of self-guided routes.

Suffolk Cycle Breaks, PO Box 82, Needham Market, Suffolk IP6 8BW. BR. Open: April to Oct. Tel: (01449) 721555. Package and self-guided tours.

Windmill Ways, 50 Bircham Road, Reepham, Kings Lynn, PE31 6SJ. Open: all year. Tel: (O1603) 871111. Cycle Hire is also available. A well-presented company specialising in East Anglian holidays.

Cycle Hire Companies

Bedfordshire:

Bedford: *Rentall,* 6 Bedford Road, Kempston, MK42 8AD. Open: all year. Tel: (01234) 353148.

Cambridgeshire:

Cambridge: *Armada Cycles,* 47 Suez Rd. Tel: (01223) 210421; *Cycle King,* 103 Cherry Hinton Rd. Open: all year. Tel: (01223) 249391; *H. Drake,* 56-60 Hills Rd, Russell St, CB2 1LA. Open: all year. Tel: (01223) 63468 Town bikes only; *Geoff's Bike Hire,* 65 Devonshire Rd, CB1 2BL. Open: all year. Tel: (01223) 65629. Afternoon and evening guided tours in summer; *Mike's Bikes,* 26-28 Mill Road. Open: CB1 2AD. Open: all year. Tel: (01223) 312591. *University Cycles,* 9 Victoria Avenue, Tel: (01223) 355517.

Holbeach: *Kens Cycles,* 80 Wignals Gate. Tel: (01406) 425572.

Huntingdon: *Grafham Water Cycling,* Marlow Park Car Park, Grafham Water, near Huntingdon, PE18 OBY. Open: all year, but not all weekdays from November to March. Tel: (01480) 812500; *Rentall,* 5 Ermine Street, PE18 6EX. Open: all year. Tel: (01480) 457555. BR.

March: *Bike Care,* 92 The Avenue, Open: All year. Tel: (01354) 660049.

Newmarket: *Armada Cycles,* Burwell. Open all year. Tel: (01638) 743108.

Peterborough: *Rentall,* 577 Lincoln Road, PE1 2PB. Tel: (01733) 51092.

Essex:

Chelmsford: *Viaduct Cycle Shop,* 38 Viaduct Rd. Open all year. BR.

Colchester: *Anglian Cycle Company,* Unit 7, Pear Tree Business Centre, Stanway, Colchester, C03 5JX. Open: all year. Tel: (01206) 563377. BR.

High Harlow: *Highway Cycles,* 7 The Rows, CM20 1BX. Open: April to October. Tel: (01279) 444141.

Maldon: *Iveson Cycles,* 120 High St, Maldon Open: All year.

Manningtree: *Chatburn Cycles,* 26 High St. Open: All year. Tel: (01206) 397032.

West Mersea: *R&A Cycles,* The Spinning Wheel, 16 Barfield Road. Tel: (01206) 384013.

Hertfordshire:

Broxbourne Meadows: *Lee Valley Cycle Hire*, Broxbourne Meadows, Mill Lane. Open: March to October. Tel: (01992) 630127. BR.

Hertford: *Highway Cycles*, 12 St Andrews Street, SG14 1JP. Open: April to October. Tel: (01992) 504548. BR.

Stevenage: *Highway Cycles*, 22/24 The Glebe, Chells, SG2 0DJ. Open: April to October. Tel: (01438) 355109. BR.

Ware: *Highway Cycles*, 35 Amwell End, SG12 9HP. BR. Open: April to October. Tel: (01920) 461448.

Norfolk:

Brancaster: *North Norfolk Cycle Hire Scheme*, The Barn, The Harbour, Brancaster Staithe. Open: July to September. Tel: (01485) 210719.

Cromer: *Trevor Medland Cycles*, 6 Brook Street, Cromer, NR27 9EY. Open: all year. Tel: (01263) 512537. BR.

Diss: *Dickleburgh Cycle Hire*, 11 Merlewood, Dickleburgh, P21 4PL. Open: all year. Tel: (01379) 741510. BR.

Great Yarmouth: *Lawfords*, 224 Northgate Street, NR30 1BG. Open: Easter to September. Tel: (01493) 842741. BR.

Norwich: *V&M Cycles*, 72a Gloucester Street, Open: All year. Tel: (01603) 632467. BR.

Thetford: *High Lodge*, Forest Centre, Thetford Forest. Open: all year. Tel: (01485) 540642.

Suffolk:

Aldeburgh: *Suffolk Cycle Hire*, 70 Franklins Road. Open: all year. Tel: (01728) 454408.

Darsham: *Byways Bicyles*, Priory Lane, IP17 3QD. Open: all year. Tel: (01728) 668764. Also offering tandem tours and accommodation. BR.

Martlesham Heath: *Pedal Power*, 15 The Square, 1P5 7SI. Open: All year. Tel: (01473) 610500.

Stutton: *Alton Water Cycle Hire*, Holbrook Road, Stutton, near Ipswich. Open: May-September daily. Other times 'phone first. Tel: (01473) 328873, (0850) 597579 (mobile).

Wrentham: *Cedar Cycles*, Tower Mills, Southwold Road, NR34 7SF. Open: all year. Tel: (01502) 75473.

EAST MIDLANDS

Includes Derbyshire, Leicestershire, Lincolnshire,
Northamptonshire, Nottinghamshire.
Tourist Information: East Midlands Tourist Board,
Exchequergate, Lincoln LN2 1PZ. Tel: (01522) 531521/3

The East Midlands is a region of contrasts. The rural lowlands of
Lincolnshire in the east, with its traditional seaside resorts of Mableth-
orpe and Skegness, seem a world apart from the high moorlands of the
Peak District. Here, the dark gritstone edges and peat moors surround in
a horseshoe shape the softer limestone landscape of the White Peak. The
land between is a blend of rurality and industrialisation, of canals and
past coalfields, of proud cities and market towns which have resisted,
but not entirely avoided, the tide of late 20th century development.

Derbyshire and particularly the Peak National Park, with its 20
million visitors per year, is renowned for cycling. There is heart-beating
stuff from Buxton to the Cat and Fiddle Inn, or a saunter along the High
Peak and Tissington trails which welcome thousands of cyclists every
year. Mountain Biking has an established base in the Peak District and
there are miles of bridleway and by-ways to follow and guide books to
help in that choice. (Try Clive Smith's 'Off-Beat Cycling' books for
starters. Both published by Sigma Press.)

For those touring England, the Peak District should not be missed, but
lonelier parts of the region offer equal pleasure. The Lincolnshire Wolds,
Northamptonshire's market towns, and Sherwood Forest are places to
cycle -as are the quiet lanes of the Vale of Belvoir, which lead to Oakham
and Rutland Water which has to be one of the most popular cycling
venues in the country.

Lincolnshire, Leicestershire and Nottinghamshire tend to be underestimated for cycling but all three authorities take an interest in providing
for the needs of the leisure cyclist. The joy of cycling hereabouts is as
much the appeal of the small historic towns such as Sleaford and
Stamford, Southwell and Uppingham as the intervening countryside.
Away from the main roads this undiscovered quarter of England has
much to offer.

COUNTRYSIDE RIDE

Tennyson Country: a Lincolnshire Cycle Ride

Joe Barker and Emma Brooks, Cyclists and Freelance Writers.

Distance: 80 miles

Terrain: an easy going two-day tour.

Maps: O.S Landranger maps 113 Grimsby and Cleethorpes and 122 Skegness.

Rail Access: Market Rasen.

Accommodation and Refreshment: there is ample accommodation in Louth, Caistor or Alford. For those who prefer to stay in one of the villages there is accommodation in Donington, Tetford and Somersby which are ideal mid-way points. There is a youth hostel at Woody's Top. Tel: Tourist Information at Louth on (01507) 609289

Cycle Hire: none on route. Nearest available at *Wheelabout Woodhall*, Woodhall Spa. Tel: (01526) 352448

The Ride

These rounded chalk hills, the Lincolnshire Wolds, inspired Lord Tennyson to write some of his greatest poetry. He described the place in terms of "calm and deep peace", an apt description to this day if you wander from the main roads. This patchwork of fields easing down to the flat coastal strip is punctuated by hamlets and villages which have not changed much despite the demands of the 20th century. Most of the route follows minor roads which, contrary to popular opinion, climb several hills but there are few steep inclines to encounter.

Seeing Places

Louth: the compact market town of Louth with its handsome Georgian houses and coaching inns is a good centre for the Wolds. The church with its impressive spire can be seen for miles around and nearby is a small museum with an unusual collection of moths and butterflies.

Somersby: birthplace of Lord Tennyson whose poetry endeared the hearts of Victorian literary society including Queen Victoria. Tennyson was Poet Laureate to her and his work was certainly influenced by his life at Somersby.

Alford: Sam Oxley's five-sailed windmill dates from the early 19th century when windmills were still in great demand for milling. This remarkable survivor can mill up to 5 tons of corn per day. Alford has built something of a reputation as a craft centre.

The Route

1. From the town centre of Louth take the A157 Lincoln Road west out of town towards Lincoln. You come to a large roundabout, part of the recently built Louth By-pass. Cross this with care, following signs for the A631 to Gainsborough. The road bears to the right and there is a gentle uphill climb followed by a fast descent through a tunnel of trees into South Elkington.

2. Continue ahead on the main road until you reach a crossroads where you should turn right towards the villages of Wold Newton and East Ravendale. Follow this road as it undulates along of the top of the Wolds, passing by the fine looking Boswell House to your left and the first of one of the many copses to be seen along the route. Ignore all turnings to the left and right as you go to Wold Newton.

3. It is not far on the route ahead to east Ravendale. At the junction with the B1203 turn right into the village, where you will see Ravendale Hall, and then take a sharp left towards Hatcliffe. This quiet road runs through woodland and over several cattle grids passing the farming complex of West Ravendale, the site of Ravendale Priory.

4. Ride on to a junction where you bear right, aiming for Beelsby as you wheel through the up-market village of Hatcliffe before the climb to Beelsby itself. Just before the latter village turn left for Croxby. About one mile along you reach a crossroads.

5. Go right here and, after Ash Holt copse, where there is a long barrow, go next left for Cuxwold. There are good views across the Lincolnshire Wolds along this section. Pass by the ancient church and hall as you keep left in this loveliest of hamlets and then ride on to Rothwell, passing Cherry Valley farms.

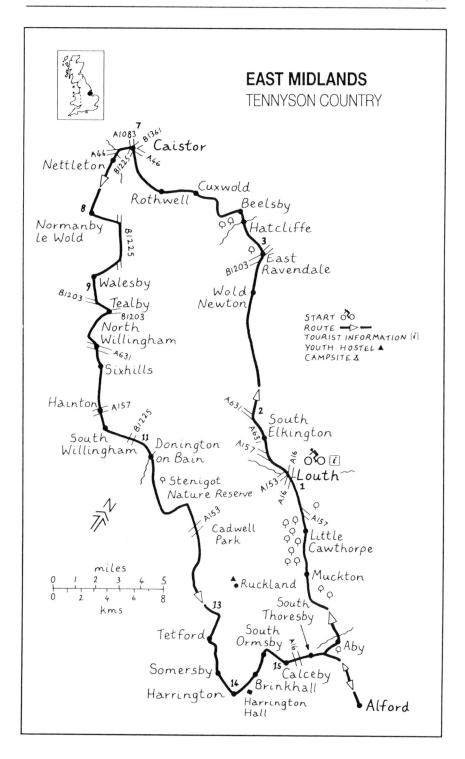

6. At the T-junction turn right into the village where you will find the charming Nickerson Arms. After a refuel, take a right turn at the next junction towards Caistor, keeping right at the following junction and then left down Whitegate Hill. At the main A46 road go straight over into the historic gap town of Caistor. Ride triumphantly into the square, in some respects not much changed since Georgian days.

7. Turn left at the square and rejoin the main A46 road towards Nettleton. In the village take a left to pass by the distinctive parish church with its striking blue clock face, engraved with distinctive gold numbers. Fork right towards Normanby Le Wold climbing out of the village up Nettleton Hill to Nettleton Top, passing large radar stations on the way.

8. On the very edge of Normanby, turn left at the junction and head towards Thorseway, ignoring another lane going right into Normanby. Pass by Top Buildings where is a long barrow nearby then go right at the next junction heading for Walesby. Ignore turnings to the left and follow the road as it bears right. At the crossroads, go right to descend into Walesby, passing near to the lonely hillside church of All Saints, known as 'The Ramblers Church' due to its nearness to the Viking Way. The walk up to the church is well worth the detour.

9. Leave the village on the Market Rasen Road (which is where you exit for rail access from the route). On the edge of the village turn left for Tealby. On reaching the B1203 turn left for Binbrook. The road climbs into Tealby. Turn right by the church through the village and by a small tea shop and general stores.

10. Leave the village and keep ahead at the junction soon to pass The Grange. Go left onto the A631 Louth Road. At the village of North Willingham turn right towards Sixhills where you keep ahead. In quick succession you travel though the villages of Hainton (where you cross the A157) and South Willingham, where you make a left turn.

11. Go ahead at the crossroads and make your way to Donington-on-Bain, ignoring the turn to the left for the lost village of Biscathorpe and a right turn for Benniworth. Those choosing to return to Louth (cut-off point) should bear first left after the bridge over the River Bain. Otherwise ride into the village where you will find The Black Horse inn, a possible overnight stop.

12. Continue through the village to Stenigot, ignoring turns left and right. Pass the parkland of Stenigot House and Moses Farm. At the junction with Manor Farm, turn left for Raithby and the peak of Red

Hill where there are wonderful views over the Lincolnshire country-side. At the crossroads turn right to Cadwell and Belchford. The road crosses the A153 road and then passes the motor racing circuit of Cadwell Park, famous for its motor cycle and touring car racing.

13. Proceed along the road, again ignoring turns to the left and right, to a cross-roads at Tetford Hill. Go left if staying overnight at Woodys Top Youth Hostel. Otherwise turn right to the beautiful village of Tetford, and the adjacent hamlet of Little London. Leave by way of the South Ormsby Road, but look for a right turning not far out of Tetford. This leads down to the Wolds hamlets of Somersby and Bag Enderby, where Tennyson once worshipped in the parish church.

14. Ride on to pass Harrington Hall and Harrington Hill where you make a continuous climb to the aptly named Brinkhill (with its "Hovis" shop and pottery) and then to South Ormsby. Turn right out of South Ormsby to Calceby where a left turn is made. Climb the steep hill by the sad ruins of an old church. Cross the staggered junction at the main A16 road and cycle to South Thoresby. In the centre of the village turn left at the T-junction. The Vine Inn offers refreshment here.

15. Proceed towards Aby and Claythorpe, passing a turn on the right to Rigsby. Take the next turn right for a worthwhile detour to Alford. Return to this same junction afterwards, but now turn right to ride through Aby, under the railway bridge to Claythorpe. Turn sharp left to pass Claythorpe Mill and onward to a junction at Authorpe where you keep left to the village of Muckton. At Authorpe Grange turn right at the crossroads.

16. Climb out to Muckton Bottom and Little Cawthorpe by a windmill. At Little Cawthorpe go right at the junction by the church. You can visit the last public house before Louth if you wish, known as The Splash and reached through a small ford where Landrovers and cycles seem to be abandoned from time to time!

17. Out of Little Cawthorpe, head onto the main A157 Legbourne to Louth Road, passing Kenwick Hall on the left. The road leads into Louth, journey's end on this tour of the Lincolnshire Wolds.

GREAT CYCLING IDEAS!

The Peak District has hundreds of off-road trails and there's good progress on routes elsewhere especially in the cities of Derby, Leicester and Nottingham allowing access into the nearby countryside. Rutland Water has to be worth the visit and the quiet lanes of Lincolnshire and Nottinghamshire are fine for cycling.

Derbyshire

Carsington Water, near Wirksworth: there is a circular ride around this recently-created and impressive reservoir. Part off-road and partly along lanes.

Cycling by Carsington Water (Chris Rushton)

Country Rides in and Around Erewash: a series of rides in the Erewash Valley. Leaflet available.

Cromford Canal: a towpath ride is available between Cromford and Whatstandwell where there is a link to the High Peak Trail at Middleton Top. 4 miles.

Derby to Elvaston Castle Cycle Route: five miles of riverside route to Elvaston Castle and Country Park.

Derby to Melbourne Cycle Route: 8 miles of off-road path using the disused Derby Canal and the Old Melbourne railway line to the historic market town.

Five Pits Trail: as its name suggests, this path runs through part of the old Derbyshire coalfield between Normanton and Tibshelf. 7.5 miles.

Goyt Valley: a 2.5 mile section of road in the upper reaches of the popular (with cars) Goyt Valley.The Goyt Valley is closed to cars on Sundays and summer weekends.

High Peak Trail: one of the longest-established cycle paths in the country, using the track-bed of the famous Cromford and High Peak railway, with its ferocious inclines. Nearly 18 miles of off-road cycling which is extremely popular.

Monsal Trail: a section of the Monsal Trail between Bakewell old railway station and Great Longstone is open to cyclists. Approximately 3 miles in length. Leaflet available.

Sett Valley Trail: a short ride (3 miles) between Hayfield old station and the outskirts of New Mills where there is a walking route around the Torrs, a beautiful gorge where mills once stood. Leaflet available.

Shipley Country Park: there are four designated rides through the country park which is situated near Heanor. Leaflet available.

Tissington Trail: another good stretch of off-road path between Ashbourne and Parsley Hay where it joins with the High Peak Trail. Leaflet available.

Trans-Pennine Trail - Hadfield to Woodhead: five miles of excellent scenery looking across the reservoirs of Crowden to the high Pennine moors from the trail. This remainder of the trail develops month by month including a link to Chesterfield.

Upper Derwent Valley: the section of road running near the water's edge from the Visitor and Cycle Hire centre at Fairholmes to Kingstree is closed to cars on Sundays and on most weekends throughout the year. This 5 mile run is complemented by a 7 mile route from Slippery Stones to Ashopton Viaduct. Leaflet available.

Cycling near Horncastle (Lincolnshire County Council)

Leicestershire

Ashby Woulds Heritage Trail: a 3-mile ride along what was once the Ashby and Nuneaton joint railway in an old coalfield area. Leaflet available.

Cycling in Leicestershire: an attractive fold-out county cycle route passing Beacon Hill and Bosworth Battlefield, Belvoir castle and Foxton Locks. An adventurous 140-mile route. Leaflet available.

Cycling around Rutland: three routes inviting you to cycle along the quieter lanes of the legendary county which refused to disappear during the last local government reorganisation. The routes link historic villages such as Great Casterton and Empingham. Small charge for leaflet.

Cycling around Rutland Water: a leaflet describing 25 miles of cycling around this waterside paradise for casual cycling.

Green Ringway, Leicester: a 20-mile waymarked circular route around Leicester, a city which is taking cyclists seriously. Leaflet available.

Lincolnshire

Cycling in North Kesteven: six cycling routes in this attractive part of Lincolnshire from the market town of Sleaford to such places as Heckington to see its famous windmill.

Lincolnshire Cycle Trails: a series of cycle routes from 11 to 29 miles which include some off-road sections but mainly uses minor roads. They include some of the county's loveliest villages and towns. Price £3 - £4. Tel: (01522) 552821.

Fossdyke Circum Navigations: three routes out of Saxilby in and around the Fossdyke navigation. Leaflet available.

Ranby Roman Road: a 7-mile cycling route based on the old Roman road.

National Cycle Museum, Lincoln: a major collection of cycles and cycling artefacts re-living the history of the bicycle. Tel: (01522) 545091.

Viking Way: designed as a long-distance walking route there are several sections where cycling is allowed such as the Ermine Street section where the way follows the old Roman Road for nearly 10 miles.

Witham Wanderings: two cycle routes from Fiskerton and Lincoln which meander around the River Witham. Leaflet available.

Wheelabout Woodhall Spa: a spa trail route which suggests 21 miles of cycle route around the small traditional spa route to Horncastle. Leaflet available.

Northamptonshire

Brampton Valley Way: a 15-mile route linking Boughton near Northampton and Market Harborough along the old rail route.

Northamptonshire Cycletours: a series of mainly road routes (but with off-road options) highlighted in 9 leaflets. Rides vary from 4 to 25 miles, including the Nene and Brampton valleys.

Nottinghamshire

Circular Rides series of leaflets which include Epperstone Park to Southwell Minster, Creswell to Carburton and Clumber to Crookford. A mixture of bridleways and lanes. Joined up they make Ducal Nottinghamshire, a 32-mile ride through the Dukeries of Nottinghamshire.

Clipstone Forest Circular Route: a six-mile forest route outlined in a leaflet "The Greenwoods of Nottinghamshire".

Dukeries Cycle Trails: a ride to Welbeck and Worksop (22 miles) or through Clumber and Sherwood (25 miles). Rides through the medieval forest of Sherwood.

Greater Nottingham Cycle Route Network Map: as to be expected of a city which held the internationally recognised Velo Conference in 1993, it has a policy of developing a cycling network which also has a leisure use. The local campaigning group, Pedals, has produced *The Pedal-Pushers Guide to Nottingham* which is essential reading. Price range: £3 - £4.

North West Cycle Routes: five cycle routes in the north and west of the county including 'The Pilgrim Fathers Route' and a D. H. Lawrence ride. Price about £2. Tel: Nottinghamshire County Council on (0115) 977 4483.

Southwell Trail: a rail path from Southwell to Bilsthorpe which runs through orchards (Southwell is the home of the Bramley apple) towards Sherwood Forest for about 8 miles. Southwell Minster and the historic central core of the town are very attractive. Lord Byron evidently lived here for a time but a little before the cycling era.

Trent Valley Cycle Routes: a series of five routes running through the quiet villages of the Trent Valley, including Sherwood Forest and the medieval strip farming village of Laxton. Routes vary from 26 to 49 miles. Price: about £2. Tel: (0115) 977 4223.

Cycle Holiday Companies

Peak Activities Ltd, Rock Lea Activity Centre, Station Road, Hathersage, S30 1DD. Open: all year. Tel: (01433) 650345. A well-established activity centre which includes adventurous cycling breaks and training courses in spectacular scenery.

Cycle Hire Companies

Derbyshire:

Ashbourne: *Cycle Hire Centre*, Mapleton Lane, DE6 2AA. Open: Open most days, March to November. Weekend opening during other months but check. Tel: (01335) 343156; *Dovedale Cycle Hire*, The Old Orchard, Thorpe, DE6 2AW. Open: all year. Tel: (01335) 29410.

Bakewell: *Noton Cycle Centre*, Over Haddon, near Bakewell. Open: all year. Tel: (01629) 814195. Also arranges cycle holidays February to November.

Buxton: *Roughguide Mountain Bike Hire*, Wellcroft Filling Station, Peak Forest, near Buxton. Open: all year. Tel: (01298) 77059. Also at *Lyme Tree Caravan Park*, Under the Viaduct, Buxton. Open: Summer only. Tel: (01298) 22988.

Carsington: *Carsington Water Cycle Hire*, Carsington water, near Ashbourne, DE6 1ST. Open: all year. Tel: (01629) 540478.

Cromford: *Middleton Top Cycle Hire*, Near Cromford. Open: Open most days April to October, several days in December and weekends at other times but check. Tel: (01629) 823204.

Derwent: *Derwent Cycle Hire*, Fairholmes, Derwent, Bamford, S30 2AQ.

Open: Open most days from March to mid-November. Weekends at other times but check. Tel: (01433) 651261.

Hayfield: *Buckingham's Mountain Bikes*, Royal Hotel. Open: all year. Tel: 0161 419 9720. Tours can be arranged; *Hayfield Cycle Hire*, Hayfield Station Picnic Site. Open: April to October. Other times closed. Tel: (01663) 746222.

Hartington: *Parsley Hay Cycle Hire*, Hartington, SK17 0DG. Open: most days from March to the end of November. Open subject to weather and staff. At other times, check. Tel: (01298) 84493.

Heanor: *Shipley Country Park Cycle Hire*, Visitor centre, Slack Lane, Heanor, Derbyshire DE7 7GX. Open: Open daily from May to August, weekends during other months, check. Tel: (01773) 719961.

Matlock: *Stanley Fearn Mountain Bike Hire*, 19 Bakewell Road, DE4 3AU. Open: all year. Tel: (01629) 582089. BR.

Monyash: *Rough Guide Mountain Bike*, The Old Smithy Tea Room, The Square, near Bakewell. Open: Summer only. Tel: (01629) 814510.

Whaley Bridge: *Open Country*, Peak District Mountain Bike Centre, 3 Market Street. Open: all year. Tel: (01663) 735020. Holidays are arranged April to September. BR.

Leicestershire:

Blaby: *Julie's Cycle Shop*, Sycamore Street, LE8 3FJ. Open: February to November. Tel: (0116) 277 0449.

Leicester: *Rentall*, 572 Melton Road, Thurmaston LE4 8BB. Open: all year. Tel: (0116) 260 1019.

Market Harborough: *George Halls Cycle Centre*, 12 Northampton Road, LE16 9HE. BR. Open: all year. Tel: (01898) 465507.

Rutland Water: *Rutland Water Cycling*, Whitwell Car Park, Rutland Water, near Oakham, LE15 8BL. Open: all year. Tel: (01780) 86705. Holidays can be arranged.

Lincolnshire:

Boston: *Nev's Cycle Centre*, 10 Church Street. Open: All year. Tel: (01205)

361560; *Oaken Cycle Hire*, Oaken Crafts Friskney Eaudyke, near Boston. Open: March to October. Tel: (01754) 820871.

East Firsby: *Lincolnshire Lanes*, Manor Farm, LN2 3DB. Open: all year. Tel: (01673) 8782158.

Grantham: *Cycle Sport UK*, 33 London Road, Grantham, Lincolnshire NG31 6EX. Open: all year. Tel: (01476) 74268. *Rentall*, 15 Springfield Road, NG31 7ED. Open: all year. Tel: (01476) 67514. BR.

Spalding: *Foreman Bridge Caravan Park*, Sutton St James. Tel: (01945) 440346; *Gibbons Cycles*, Winsover Road, PE11 1HA. Open: all year. Tel: (01775) 722050. BR.

Woodhall Spa: *Wheelabout Woodhall* (East Lindsey District Council), Jubilee Park, Stixwould Road, Woodhall Spa. Open: April until September. Tel: (01526) 352448.

Northamptonshire:

Oundle: *Valley Bike Hire*, 5a West Street, PE8 4EJ. Open: all year, but not Monday or Tuesday. Tel: (01832) 275381.

Nottinghamshire:

Clipstone Forest: *Bunny's Bikes*, Forest Centre. Open: Summer only. Tel: (0115) 947 2713.

Clumber Park: *Clumber Park Cycle Hire*, Clumber Park Estate, Nottinghamshire. Open: Easter to the end of September and Winter weekends, weather permitting. Tel: (01909) 476592.

Nottingham: *Rentall*, 35A Nottingham Road, Daybrook, NG5 6JW. Open: all year. Tel: (0115) 920 9837; *Bunny's Bikes*, Carrington Street, NG1 7SE. Open: all year. Tel: (0115) 947 2713. BR.

THE NORTH WEST

Includes Cheshire, Greater Manchester, Lancashire, Merseyside and High Peak District (See Derbyshire in East Midlands section for the latter).
Tourist Information: North West Tourist Board, Swan House, Swan Meadow Road, Wigan Pier WN3 5BB.
Tel: (01942) 821222

From the dairy lands of South Cheshire to the wild hills of the Trough of Bowland, the North West has a varying landscape. Divided though it may be by the two conurbations of Greater Manchester and Merseyside the surrounding counties provide well for the recreational cyclist. Not that the great Victorian cities of Manchester and Liverpool are a lost cause -far from it. There are initiatives in both cities to develop the thread of old railway and canal towpaths for traffic free cycling and there are good routes in the Daisy Nook and Saddleworth areas already. Manchester is now also home to a major international velodrome.

Cheshire's high hills give way reluctantly to the Cheshire Plain, which despite its name is not entirely level, but punctuated by sandstone edges as at Alderley and Frodsham. There is also scope to ride between market towns and villages through Cheshire parklands to admire the Hall at Gawsworth or Tatton. South of Chester and Crewe is a myriad of quieter lanes leading to the ruins of Beeston castle and Peckforton hill, to the elegant Cholmondley Castle and the market place of Malpas. This quarter beckons the touring cyclist.

Lancashire is very much a county of contrasts from the brash seaside resorts of Blackpool and Morecambe with low lying pastures of the Fylde to the changing cotton mill towns of the Ribble Valley and Rossendale which have always cherished access to the West Pennine Moors. But the main attractions are the back roads through the wild Forest of Bowland and fells of north Lancashire.

There are excellent cycleways in both Cheshire and Lancashire and dozens of opportunities for gentler off-road cycling using disused railway tracks and country parks. Beyond these there are still wilder parts to satisfy the need for fierce climbs.

105

COUNTRYSIDE RIDE.

Cycle and See the Staffordshire Moorlands

A two-day ride through the Western Peakland by Angie Rann, Senior Tourism Officer, Staffordshire Moorlands.

Distance: 38 miles.

Terrain: strenuous. Preferably a touring bike but all types of bike may be used.

Map: O.S. Landranger maps 118 The Potteries and 119 Buxton.

Rail Access: Macclesfield Railway Station.

Accommodation and Refreshment: there is accommodation in Macclesfield and throughout the route. Contact Tourist Information at Leek on (01538) 381000. Refreshment available throughout route.

Cycle Hire: Nearest hire is at The Groundwork Trust in Bollington, near Macclesfield. Tel: (01625) 572681.

The Ride

The ride soon leaves the streets of Macclesfield behind to run through the quiet lanes of Cheshire to lesser-known parts of the Peak District. Cross the gushing waters of the infant River Dane to the Staffordshire Moorlands, wild and yet welcoming with roadside farms and inns.

The mystical shapes of Ramshaw Rocks and The Roaches, the haunting beauty of the upper Dane and the water and woods of Macclesfield Forest provide a contrast throughout the route which could be done in a day by those who are experienced riders in hill terrain. Otherwise take your time and make a two-day run out of the route.

Seeing Places

Macclesfield: Macclesfield's heritage is silk and the Silk Heritage Centre and Macclesfield Silk Mill exhibit the town's manufacturing history. The flowing waters of the Bollin and a damp climate suited textiles well and from the medieval core of the town above Waters Green Macclesfield developed as a mill centre.

The Roaches: the series of millstone grit outcrops alongside Five Clouds, Hen Cloud and Ramshaw Rocks make up an area much loved by climbers and walkers. The ride passes Tittesworth reservoir, a superb facility with a visitor centre and exhibition, café, nature trail and children's playground, and the Moorlands villages of Meerbrook and Upper Hulme.

Flash: this is England's highest village at 1518 feet above sea level; there may be higher hamlets, but Flash qualifies as a village with its post office! It also has England's highest church and is host to one of the highest pubs in the land. In past times, Flash was a centre for counterfeiting until the Government of the day despatched a crack team of constables from Chester to stop the practice. The term "flashy" still survives.

Gradbach: in the upper reaches of the Dane is the hamlet of Gradbach where a mill once produced fine silk. It is now a youth hostel. Dismount here for a short trek to the mysterious Lud's Church, a natural rocky chasm, nearly 50 feet high and yet only a few feet wide, where religious dissenters met for clandestine services.

Be prepared on this route for several climbs and equally fast descents where steady braking should be used to hold speed down. The reward is a succession of excellent views and the sheer sense of the wilderness along sections of the ride. Be prepared in Winter for this is high ground and the weather can become inclement within short time spans.

The Route

1. Turn left from Macclesfield Railway station along Sunderland Street and take the second left up Brook Street to cross the new inner ring road. Take the first right, Swettenham Street, after the Wharf Public House and before the Hovis Mill (the home of the famous loaf in earlier times).

2. Cycle the length of Swettenham Street, turn left at the junction and ride up to the next junction ahead where you go right. Bear left at the Navigation pub and then proceed ahead at the crossroads along Black Road. This becomes Gunco Lane and winds its way to Byrons Lane. Turn left here.

3. The route climbs steadily out of Macclesfield to pass beneath the

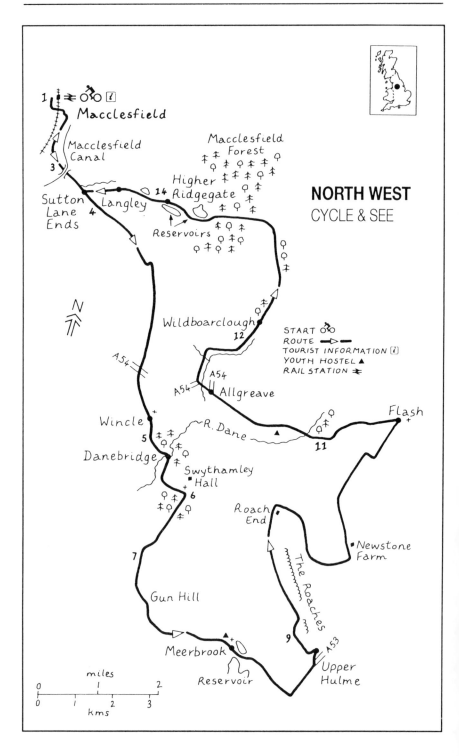

1 Macclesfield

Macclesfield Canal

3

Sutton Lane Ends

Langley 4

14 Higher Ridgegate

Macclesfield Forest

Reservoirs

NORTH WEST
CYCLE & SEE

N

Wildboarclough
12

A54

A54

A54 Allgreave

START
ROUTE
TOURIST INFORMATION [i]
YOUTH HOSTEL ▲
RAIL STATION ⇌

Wincle
5

Danebridge

R. Dane

Flash

11

Swythamley
Hall

6

Roach End

Newstone Farm

7

Gun Hill

The Roaches

9

A53

Meerbrook

Reservoir

Upper Hulme

miles
0   1   2
0   1   2   3
kms

impressive arch of the Sutton aqueduct and by a house which bears a plaque to commemorate the brilliant canal engineer, James Brindley. Take the next left and follow this to an awkward corner by the Church Inn, awkward as you are making a right turn and another steeper climb.

4. This now becomes a much quieter route up to the Hanging Gate public house. Ignore the three turnings on the left to Langley and save yourself for a climb up to the pub. Keep ahead along the ridge ignoring a left turn to Wildboarclough and another on the right. You come to a crossroads at the main A54 road. Cross this and cycle onward to Wincle where the road dips steeply with the little church to your left.

5. The road rises again and then descends to Danebridge passing by the Ship Inn. Cross the bridge and the road rises to the right. Take a left turn at the next junction following the Swythamley Hall park boundary wall on your left.

6. At the Hall's entrance gates bear right. At the next junction, signposted to Leek, go left and at Gun End Farm (splendid refreshments here) keep right. Bear around to the left at Hawksley Farm.

7. You come to a triangular junction where you follow the left-hand road signposted to Meerbrook, a long climb up the shoulders of Gun Hill, an isolated place where villains were once hung, drawn and quartered. Perhaps, it is best to pedal past this spot but do pause to take in the views across Cheshire while you catch your breath. There's an even longer and fast descent to the village of Meerbrook but watch for cars here.

8. Pass the youth hostel and bear right by the Lazy Trout pub to Tittesworth where access is to the right. If not calling, keep ahead to cycle up to the main road at Blackshaw Moor by the Three Horseshoes public house. Go left along a busy but short section. The road dips and then on the long haul up go left, signposted to Upper Hulme. Keep left into the village (unless calling at Ye Olde Rock Inn which is just on the right) and through the works.

9. The road climbs and levels, as it flanks the Roaches. Ignore turnings to the left and right. Keep straight on as signposted to Royal Cottage up to Roach End. The road is gated so cars tend to be deterred. Swing right and descend. Continue past a right-hand junction and keep straight on to Hazel Barrow. At the T-junction here turn left.

10. Follow this road to another junction at Goldsitch Moss where you turn right, as signposted to Flash, and go straight across the crossroads. At the next junction go right to climb up to the village. Make

a sharp left turn by the church and by the New Inn. There's a steep descent here and pump your brakes a little harder if you are stopping off at a farm here for a cup of tea or ice-cream.

11. Turn right at the junction for Gradbach and Allgreave. There's a detour here for Gradbach Youth Hostel (which is signposted) and a walk to Lud's Church. Otherwise, keep ahead over the Dane and climb. You pass by an old farm cum inn, The Eagle and Child (a stone sign remains over the door); it is no longer licensed and was, until recently, a popular café for cyclists. Arrive at the main A54 road by the Rose and Crown pub. Turn left to dip down the hillside and then go right for Wildboarclough.

12. Follow the road ahead through the village and up the valley, a gentle climb for the most part. After nearly two miles, go left for Macclesfield Forest and Langley. It is a hard climb up the hillside to the watershed but then turn left to run through the forest.

13. Be warned: the road is steep and, in places, narrow - so keep your speed down. The ride through the woodland and by the reservoirs is excellent. Pass by a visitor centre and then keep right to run along Ridgegate Reservoir and left at The Leather's Smithy public house.

14. Drop down into Langley and ahead to the Church Inn where you regain your outward route back to Macclesfield.

Great Cycling Ideas

If you can be tempted away from the Western Peak, try the softer landscape of South Cheshire. Otherwise, the Lancashire Cycleway offers a chance to discover some of the wilder parts of the North West.

Cheshire

Cheshire Cycleway: a 135-mile waymarked circular route which links the softer landscape of South Cheshire to Cheshire's high ground by way of the Cheshire Plain. Leaflet available. Small Charge. Tel: Cheshire County Council (01244) 602424.

Delamere Forest Guide: a map and guide illustrate off-road routes (about 3 miles) through the ancient Forest of Delamere which is a great introduction to this mid-Cheshire park.

Middlewood Way: a well-established railway path which links Maccles-field to Marple (11 miles) on the very edge of the Peak District with a potential for diverting onto local lanes. Leaflet available.

Trans-Pennine Trail: one 5-mile section of the trail is available between Warrington and Heatley and another 5-mile stretch from Widnes to Warrington. (See South Yorkshire for details of the Trans Pennine Trail).

Greater Manchester

Bike It Manchester... City Cycle Routes: leaflet explaining routes for cyclists in the city which is useful for those visiting the city centre.

Bike Rides in Greater Manchester: a series of bike rides throughout Greater Manchester including Dunham Town, Reddish Vale,Salford and Saddleworth. Small charge per leaflet. Published by the Cycling Project for The North West.

Medlock Valley Bridle & Mountain Bike route: an 18-mile route from Daisy Nook to Bishop Park developed by the Greater Manchester Cycling Project.

Uppermill to Stalybridge Railway Path: a six-mile route through Sad-dleworth. Leaflet available.

Lancashire

Cycle Rides: two route cards describing routes from Lever Park and Rivington in the West Pennine Moors. Small charge.

Lancashire Cycleway: southern and northern loops meet at Whalley in the Ribble Valley. The 250-mile waymarked route has been devised by the County Council to reflect the different landscapes of Lancashire including the Fylde coast, Arnside and Lune Valley, Bowland Fells, Pennine Moors and West Lancashire Plain. Mainly on minor roads which introduce the cyclist to Lancashire at its best. Tel: Lancashire County Council on (01772) 263536

Lancaster to Morecambe Railway Path: three miles of path between the historic centre of Lancaster and seaside resort, Morecambe.

Lancaster Cycleways: railway paths out of Lancaster through the historic dock quarter and along the banks of the River Lune. Leaflet available.

Pedal Power: four cycle rides in and around Blackburn with an unusual grading system, the 6-mile "Bunny Run" to the 25 mile "Hardriders Run".

Merseyside

Cheshire Lines Path: railway path from Maghull to Ainsdale, ideal for watching birdlife. 10 miles.

Liverpool Loop Line: a 10-mile railway path between Halewood (home of the famous car plant) and Aintree (home of the famous race-course).

North Coast Park, Wirral: a coastal route is being developed out of New Brighton towards Hoylake - approximately 5 miles. Cycling is permitted on the Wirral Way (horse ride) between West Kirby and Parkgate.

Cycle Holiday Companies

Freewheel Cycle Tours, 4 Chapel Close, West Bradford, Clitheroe BB7 4TH. Open: all year. Self-led cycle tours. Tel: (01200) 442069.

Cycle Hire Companies

Cheshire:

Bollington: *Groundwork Trust Cycle Hire centre*, Adelphi Mill Gate Lodge, Grimshaw Lane, SK10 5JD. Open: Easter to September at weekends and Bank Holidays. Daily throughout July and August. Tel: (01625) 572681.

Chester: *Davies Bros (Cycles) Ltd*, 6-8 Cuppin Street, CH1 2BN. Open: June to October (01244) 319204. BR.

Delamere: *Groundwork Trust Cycle Hire*, Discovery Centre, Linmere. Open: Easter to September at weekends and Bank Holidays. Daily throughout July and August. Tel: (01625) 572681. BR.

Farndon: *South Cheshire Cycle Hire*, Meadow View Farm, Crewe Lane South, CH3 6PH. Open: all year, but please confirm by 'phone before travelling. Tel: (01829) 271242.

Tatton: *Groundwork Trust Cycle Hire*, Tatton Park, near Knutsford. Open:

Tarporley, Cheshire (Chris Rushton)

Easter to September at weekends and Bank Holidays. Daily during July and August. Tel: (01625) 572681.

Greater Manchester:

Bury: *Biking Cycles*, 63 Bolton Road West, Ramsbottom. Tel: (01706) 827477.

Offerton: *Bednall Cycle Hire*, 11 Salcombe Road, Offerton SK2 5AG. Open: all year. Tel: 0161 477 4493.

Lancashire:

Clitheroe: *Pedal Power*, Waddington Road. Open: 6 days a week, all year. Tel: (01200) 22066; *Clitheroe Cycle Hire*, 63 Edisford Road. Tel: (01200) 23482.

Horwich: *D Tours*, 49 Hope Street North, BL6 7LL. Open: all year. Tel: (01204) 699460.

YORKSHIRE AND HUMBERSIDE

Includes the counties of Humberside, North, South and West Yorkshire.
Tourist Information: Yorkshire and Humberside Tourist Board, 312 Tadcaster Road, York YO2 2HF.
Tel: (01904) 707961

The eastern coast of Humberside from Flamborough to Spurn Head and the small towns of Beverley (famous for its Minster) and Hornsea (for its pottery) make for great rides from the port of Kingston upon Hull. There is also an area to the north west between Beverley and Market Weighton where a network of lanes leading into the Yorkshire Wolds, also holds appeal to the cyclist.

The historic city of York, its narrow streets bustling with visitors making their way to York Minster, is a port of call if only to call at Betty's for a taste of Yorkshire Curd cake. Only stay a while, for North Yorkshire has so much beauty within close proximity with a mix of off-road and back routes to satisfy all comers.

It is also where you will find two areas of outstanding scenery, the North York Moors and Yorkshire Dales National Parks. The latter is characterised by its limestone scenery and great dales such as Wensleydale and Wharfedale. Here monastic ruins at Bolton, Fountains and Jervaulx melt into the surrounding beauty. The North York Moors are different. The high level moorland plateaux plummet dramatically into wooded dales some of which flow to the Humber and others to the Esk and the North Sea.

The South Pennines are often forgotten but several authorities have worked to provide off-road routes for mountain bikers, especially in Calderdale where the narrow sided valleys give way to moorland described so deftly by the Brönte sisters. Further south, the hills are less well-known except for honeypots such as Holmfirth, but the Trans-Pennine trail through the Woodhead Valley into South Yorkshire and Humberside will be a superb addition for the cyclist when complete.

COUNTRYSIDE RIDE

Riding High Over the North York Moors

Bill Breakell, Tourism Officer, North York Moors National Park.

Distance: 36 miles.

Terrain: Moderately strenuous. Suitable for mountain bikes or hybrids.

Map: O.S. Landranger Map 94 Whitby.

Rail Access: Castleton Moor on the line to Whitby.

Refreshment and Accommodation: there are scores of places to stay along the route - camping barns, farmhouses, bed and breakfast, hotels and inns. There are shops cum post offices and public houses in Castleton, Glaisdale, Rosedale and Danby. Contact: North Yorks Moors National Park on (01287) 660654 or (01439) 70173/70657.

Cycle Hire: The Purple Mountain, Applegarth Tel: (01287) 660539

The Ride

Eight hundred years ago St Ailred, the Abbot of Rievaulx Abbey described the moors as offering "a marvellous freedom from the tumult of the world." With a bike and a couple of days to spare, you can share that freedom.

The 36-mile route takes you on a journey through some of Britain's most spectacular scenery: following prehistoric trackways across heather moors, dropping down into peaceful hamlets which once thundered with industry, crossing salmon rivers by ancient bridges.

The ride is set in the heart of the 554 square mile North York Moors National Park and is a superb way to discover why the area has long been a favourite for monks, poets and all who relish peace, tranquillity and superb landscape.

The Moors rise to almost 1400 feet and there are some steep climbs out of Castleton, Commondale and Rosedale. About a third of the route is on non-metalled tracks and bridleways, the rest is on minor roads.

Although never more than six miles from a village, the moors can be inhospitable in poor weather, which can come on with little warning. Carry warm and waterproof clothing and be prepared to drop down into the valley if the going gets tough.

The ride could be undertaken in one day by those who are keen to clock up a fitness rating but it is far better to take a couple of days over the route and enjoy the scenery at leisure.

Yorkshire Dales: Dover Hill with Swaledale beyond (Roy Taylor)

Seeing Places

The joy of the ride is the contrast between dale and moorland, and the quiet North Yorkshire villages which were anything but in the last century.

Castleton: is named after its Norman castle. Originally a wooden structure on an earthen mound, it was rebuilt several times before being abandoned in the 14th century in favour of Danby Castle, (birthplace of Katherine Parr - the last of Henry VIII's wives), which you pass later on the ride. Danby Court Leet still meets here annually when the "affearors" and "pinders" levy fines on those that have breached

117

centuries-old customs for managing the commons and moors of the manor.

The present Castleton "castle" is modern having replaced 18th and 19th century buildings. Despite its medieval origins the village was considered new in 1712 and most of the houses date from the 19th century, when it became the centre of rural life for the northern dales.

It hosted an important cheese fair and the traders who walked here could rely on good service from some 17 shoemakers who carried on their trade in the village. Travel became a little easier with the coming of the railway in 1861, but it took over five years to build the line to Grosmont just a dozen miles down the valley - "It is a devil of a country" said the engineer, explaining the delay to his directors.

Commondale: a small hamlet which once produced bricks, tiles and chimney pots as well as decorative pottery. The works were finally demolished in the late 1950s. Half hidden in the surrounding moorland lie ancient pannier-ways, ditches which once marked the boundaries of medieval deer parks and literally hundreds of bronze age burial mounds.

Danby Beacon: is almost 1000 feet above sea level and commands a panoramic view of moorland routes and the coast. During Napoleonic times a soldier was stationed at the beacon ready to raise the alarm should the enemy invade. The site was so isolated that he got special dispensation to have his wife with him in the hastily constructed stone hut. The blazing beacon would have mustered the 190 men of Danby parish (with their 38 draft horses, 15 waggons and 16 carts) in defence of their homes, as one writer recounts:

"If better weapons are not provided, they will take their threshing instruments to defend his majesty and their own property.".

Glaisdale: Was a noisy, smokey, bustling place with blast furnaces, huge chimneys (one was 252 feet high), drift mines, deep shafts, a narrow gauge railway with tunnels and incline. No doubt there was hard drinking after a hot day at the furnace. The church commissioners pulled down one hostelry which, they claimed, was squatting in the vicarage grounds. The evicted owner built his new inn a few yards away and named it "The Mitre" out of spite. But mine host had barely started serving when the ironworks closed, forcing many of his customers to go west, some making the short trip to Middlesbrough, others a journey across the Atlantic to America. The hamlet is one of the quietest corners these days.

Rosedale Abbey: Like Glaisdale, Rosedale had its industrial glory during the last century. Between 1851 and 1871 the population grew five-fold. The iron company built depots, terraced houses and a lecture room, which was soon pressed into service as a hospital to treat the injuries sustained in the mines. After extracting millions of tons of ironstone, the mines closed in 1926 but the ruins are of such national significance that a preservation programme is being carried out by the National Park Authority. The village is named after a Cistercian Priory of which few remains are to be seen. But the tranquil name aptly describes this pretty village, sheltered by the surrounding hills.

The view from above Rosedale Abbey (Les Lumsdon)

The Route

1. The route starts at Castleton (Castleton Moor BR is on the route). Turn off the main road (Church Street/High Street) into Station Road, signposted to Guisborough. The road curves round the motte of the Norman castle to leave the village. Bridge the River Esk, go under the railway and begin to ascend the hill (but be assured that what goes up must come down).

2. Climb the hill and where the road sweeps up to the right, take the

119

unsurfaced track straight ahead (signposted bridleway) which leads gently downhill towards the village of Commondale. Along this section as elsewhere on the ride you will notice lines of large flat stones forming a paved causeway. These are the pannier-ways which criss-cross the moors, and have for thousands of years, provided routes for monks, soldiers, smugglers and tradesmen.

3. After the farm houses of Box Hall, Cobble Hall and Foul Green you rejoin a surfaced road for the last few yards into Commondale village. Look for the red brick houses of Ness Terrace, named after one of the owners of the brick, tile and pottery works which once dominated the village.

4. At the Cleveland Inn, turn right and head up the hill to pass the village hall, school and church, all of which are built in local brick. Climb up Sand Hill which is steep and you'll no doubt have to pause awhile to look back at the peaceful hamlet amid the sea of heather moors.

5. The road continues to White Cross, one of several moorland crosses to be seen on the ride. Like most crosses, White Cross has served several purposes: as a guidepost for travellers, as a reminder of early Christianity, and as a boundary stone.

6. Cross the road at the junction and proceed on the unmade track across Danby Low Moor for just over two miles. It may be muddy and rough but this is moorland territory at its best. When you meet the tarmac road go right towards Danby. Here are three mounds collectively known as Robin Hood's Butts. According to tradition, this is where the outlaw is said to have practised firing his arrows. They are, in reality, Bronze Age burial chambers with a tell-tale hollow of a "robber's pit" in the middle showing that they were the subject of Victorian curiosity and excavation.

7. After half a mile in the direction of Danby, turn left towards Danby Beacon. The site of the beacon happens to be another burial mound. At the beacon, follow the unmade track over the moors towards Lealholm.

8. After a mile and a half look for the track on the right heading downhill until you reach a tarmac road. Head straight on towards Lealholm. At the next T-junction turn right (signposted to Lealholm) and then after about 30 metres turn left along Lealholmside.

9. Follow the track which progressively drops down to the river after Hill House farmyard. After the river crossing (the footbridge is drier than the ford) follow the track uphill to Glaisdale.

10. In the village cross the main road, and straight across, follow the

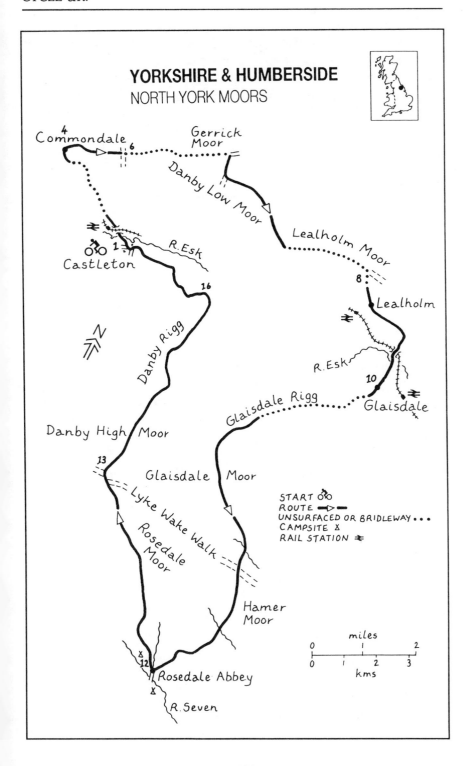

YORKSHIRE & HUMBERSIDE
NORTH YORK MOORS

Commondale 4
6
Gerrick Moor
Danby Low Moor
Lealholm Moor
R. Esk
Castleton 1
16
8
Lealholm
Danby Rigg
R. Esk
10
Glaisdale
Glaisdale Rigg
Glaisdale
Danby High Moor
13
Glaisdale Moor
Lyke Wake Walk
Rosedale Moor
Hamer Moor
12
Rosedale Abbey
R. Seven

START
ROUTE
UNSURFACED OR BRIDLEWAY •••
CAMPSITE ✕
RAIL STATION

miles
0   1   2
0   1   2   3
kms

road onto Glaisdale Rigg. The road gradually becomes a track but after a couple of miles you will join a road which you follow to the junction with the Egton to Rosedale road.

11. Turn right to pass the site of Hamer House (once a wayside inn) with its old coal pits and continue to descend to the village of Rosedale Abbey, a good place to stop for refreshment or recovery.

12. Leave by the road heading for Castleton as it climbs back onto the spine of the North Yorks Moors. After some four miles, almost on the top of the hill, is Loose Howe, a bronze age burial mound which was excavated in 1937 and found to contain the remains of a body in an oak canoe with cloak, shoes, leggings and bronze dagger.

13. After the road levels out, pause at the junction with a minor road. Look along the ridge to the left and a trio of moorland crosses can be seen - White Cross (known also as Fat Betty), Old Ralph and Young Ralph, the latter being the symbol of the North York Moors National Park. Take the road on the right into Little Fryup Dale. It gets its name from the Danish Fryga's Op (Fryga's Opening). Down this very same road came King Edward II and his retinue to lodge at Danby Castle over 600 years ago. It was something of a spectacle for the folk of Fryup not used to such pomp and pageantry.

14. The road drops down to Fairy Cross Plain, where it is said that locals used to watch the fairies dancing around Pincushion Hill at midnight. Follow the road along the valley side to Danby Castle. Just beyond turn right and follow the road down to the 13th century Duck Bridge over the Esk.

15. Once over the bridge turn left, go under the railway bridge and ride on to the National Park Visitor Centre, situated in a former shooting lodge. It houses an exhibition, tea rooms, information centre and toilets. Follow the road through to Danby village (although properly known as Dale End) and then turn left to Ainthorpe.

16. On leaving Danby you can see, to the right of the bridge, Danby Mill where the wheel and machinery have been carefully restored so that flour and meal can be ground again. The road continues through Ainthorpe, past Danby school and returns to Castleton.

GREAT CYCLING IDEAS!

Wherever you travel in this region you will not be far from an adventuresome ride into spectacular North Country scenery which we have tended to take for granted through the years. Humberside offers gentler cycling but elsewhere expect climbs and sharp descents.

Humberside

Circular Cycle Routes: a 25-card pack which includes several rail trails in Humberside.

Hudson Way: an 11-mile route from Beverley to Market Weighton.

Market Weighton to Bubwith Cycle Path: a 12-mile countryside route.

Hornsea Rail Trail: an 11-mile railpath from Hull to Hornsea.

Withernsea Branch railway path: the price range for the pack is £2 - £3. Tel: (01482) 884206.

North Yorkshire

Cropton Forest: an off-road route from Levisham railway station on the North Yorks Moors railway into the forest.

Cycling in the North York Moors Forest: a leaflet explaining both road and off-road cycling opportunities in forests hereabouts. Small charge.

Ryedale Mountain Bike Routes: a series of four leaflets available from Ryedabike which explore the countryside around and about Malton. Small charge per leaflet. Tel: Ryedabike (01653) 692835.

York Cycle Route Map: a good map for the visitor wishing to travel around York by bike.

Yorkshire Dales Cycleway: 121 miles of exceptional scenery in the Yorkshire Dales weaving its way into some lesser-known dales as well as popular haunts such as Malham and Dent.

Scarborough to Whitby Railpath: 18 miles of splendid scenery including Robin Hood's Bay on this attractive off-road route between seaside resorts.

York to Selby Cycle Path: this Sustrans built path leaves the banks of the Ouse in York to run through the race-course before heading for the old East Coast main line route to Selby. 15 miles. Leaflet available.

Trans Pennine Trail: the Howden to Selby section is now complete. 10 miles of traffic-free cycling.

South Yorkshire

Rother Valley Country Park: 4 miles of off-road cycling in this pleasant country park.

Rotherham Round Rides Cycle Routes: a series of six circular cycle routes which combine into an all-day ride of 40 miles.

Trans-Pennine Trail: Silkstone - Wombwell section available. 6 miles of traffic-free cycling.

West Yorkshire

Mountain Bike Trails-Upper Calder Valley: short and long routes mapped out by Calderdale Council in an attractive leaflet featuring starts from Hardcastle Crags and Mytholmroyd. Small charge.

West Yorkshire County Cycle Route: 150-mile route around West Yorkshire, mainly on back lanes but short sections on bridleways. The eastern half is fairly level, but the western quarter needs more pedal power to rise into the South Pennine hills. Small charge.

Cycle Holiday Companies

Bike It!, *Mountain Bike Hire*, Gales House, YO6 6HT. Open: all year. Tel: (01751) 431258.

Discovery Travel, 12 Towthorpe Road, Haxby, YO3 3ND. Open: all year. Tel: (01904) 766564.

Cycle Hire Companies

Humberside:

Brigg: *Regal Cycles*, 4 Wrawby Rd. Open: All year. Tel: (01652) 652924.

Goole: *John Donoghue Raleigh Cycle Hire*, 50 Pasture Rd, Tel: (01405) 762331.

North Yorkshire:

Boroughbridge: *Karbitz*, High Street. Open: All year. Tel: (01423) 324085.

Castleton: *The Purple Mountain*, Applegarth. Open: All year. Tel: (01287) 660539.

Gargrave: *Dave Ferguson Bikes*, 48 High St. Tel: (01756) 748030; *Wilds Country Store*, 27 High Street, BD23 3RA. Open: all year. Tel: (01756) 749476. BR.

Grassington: *Pletts Barn Mountain Bikes*, Pletts Barn, Garrs Lane, BD23 5AT. Open: all year. Tel: (01756) 752266.

Harrogate: *John Donoghue Raleigh Cycle Centre*, 41-43 High St, Starbeck. Open: All Year Tel: (01423) 883184. BR; *Spa Cycles*, 1 Wedderburn Road, HG2 7HQ. Open: all year. Tel: (01423) 887003. BR.

Holmfirth: *Super Cycles*, 201 Lockwood Rd. Open: All year. Tel: (01484) 512825.

Horton in Ribblesdale: *Three Peaks Mountain Bikes*, Studfold House, BD24 0ER. Open: all year. Tel: (01729) 860200. Accommodation available for cycling breaks. BR.

Ingleton: *Richards Cycles*, The Square. Open: All year. Tel: (01524) 241094.

Kettlewell: *The Garage*, BD23 1RQ. Open: all year. Tel: (01756) 760225.

Pickering: *Taylors Cycles*, Hungate. Open: All year. Tel: (01751) 472143.

Richmond: *Arthur Caygill Cycles*, Gallowfields Trading Estate, DL10 6PE. Open: all year. Tel: (01748) 825469; *Punch Bowl Inn*, Low Row, Upper Swaledale, DL11 6PF. Open: all year. Tel: (01748) 86233. Offers accommodation which is ideal for families and groups.

Rosedale Abbey: *Bell End Farm Cottages*, Rosedale Abbey, near Pickering. Open: all year. Tel: (01751) 417431. Quality self catering accommodation also available.

Skipton: *Eric Burgess Cycles*, Water Street, Open: All Year. Tel: (01756) 794386; *Dave Ferguson Cycles*, Brook Street. Tel: (01756) 795367.

Swainby: *Blue Sky Leisure*, 64 High Street, DL6 3EG. Open: all year. Tel: (01642) 700754.

York: *Bike Busters*, Fishergate. Tel: (01860) 785839; *Cycle Scene*, 2 Radcliffe Street, Burton Stone Lane, YO3 6EN. BR. Open: all year. Tel: (01904) 653286; *York Cycle Works*, 14-16 Lawrence Street. Open: April to September. Tel: (01904) 626664. BR.

Rickshaw rides from Peter Burgess are available in the city - contact Tourist Information for details.

South Yorkshire:

Barnsley: *Cycosport*, 25 Doncaster Road, Barnsley, S70 1TH. Open: all year. Tel: (01226) 204020. Mobile mountain bike hire in South Yorkshire and the Peak District, 'phone to hire. BR.

Rotherham: *Jezo Mountain Bikes*, 34 Silvermoor Drive, Ravenfield, S65 4QF. Open: all year. Tel: (01709) 531799. BR.

West Yorkshire:

Bingley: *Keith Lambert,* 108 Main Street. Open: All year. Tel: (01274) 560605. BR.

Ilkley: *Wharfedale Cycle Depot,* 32 Leeds Road. Tel: (01943) 607957.

Halifax: *Cycle Gear*, New Road. Tel: (01422) 344602.

Keighley: *Aire Valley Cycles*, 102-104 East Parade, BD21 5H2. Open: all year but notice preferred in Winter months. Tel: (01535) 610839. BR.

Leeds: *Watson Cairns & Co Ltd*, Lower Briggate, LS1 6NG. Open: all year. Tel: (0113) 245 8081. BR; *Two Wheels Good,* 35 Call Lane. Tel: (0113) 245 6867.

Mytholmroyd: *D.C. Mansfield*, 9 New Road. Open: All Year Tel: (01422) 884397. BR.

Sowerby Bridge: *Cycle Gear*, 61-63 Wharfe St. Open: All year. Tel: (01422) 831676.

Wetherby: *Alan Kays Cycles*, Scott Lane. Open: All Year Tel: (01937) 62682.

CUMBRIA

This includes the Lake District and the Eden Valley
Tourist Information: Cumbria Tourist Board, Ashleigh,
Holly Road, Windermere, Cumbria LA23 2AQ. Tel:
(01539) 444444

Those most famous of Lakes, Ullswater and Windermere, their icy waters rippling against a backcloth of imposing mountains, have attracted visitors *en masse* since the time of Wordsworth. The beauty and grandeur of the area are undeniable and, not surprisingly, the Lake District National Park seeks to maintain the balance between countryside access and conservation. Mountain biking is very popular and it is best to take advice from a local hirer as to the acknowledged routes which run through oak woodlands to higher fells.

But Cumbria is far more than Lakeland. It is a large rural county where you can leave fellow visitors behind. The respite is sorely needed for the roads in the central area are saturated by cars in summer and very unpleasant for cycling. Western Cumbria, the coastal stretch between Barrow in Furness and the Solway Firth is more pleasant except for the nuclear power plant at Sellafield. It is also possible to ride into the Western reaches of the Cumbrian mountains from Ravenglass and Broughton in Furness.

A firm favourite of many is to ride the eastern fringe of the county through the Eden Valley, from Penrith to Appleby to join the Settle to Carlisle railway or down to Sedbergh on the Cumbrian cycleway. These are all superb places for cycling as you can weave your way along back lanes between stations on the line. To the north lies Talkin Tarn Country Park and Hadrians Wall and miles of riding along the very quiet borderlands.

Furness is the lowland of Cumbria where the Southern Lakeland gives way to the gentler pastures of the peninsula to Walney Island and Morecambe Bay. The routes along the coastline are rewarding if you choose a quiet time to ride otherwise it is best to select routes a few miles inland.

COUNTRYSIDE RIDE

Ennerdale and Loweswater

Distance: 64 miles.

Terrain: Moderately strenuous. Preferably a two-day tour.

Map: O.S. Landranger 89 West Cumbria.

Rail Access: Whitehaven.

Accommodation and Refreshment: the route is well blessed with public houses and there is accommodation in Cockermouth, Whitehaven and various villages. Contact Tourist Information on (01946) 695678. There are youth hostels at Cockermouth and Ennerdale.

Cycle Hire: Track and Trail, Frizington. Tel: (01946) 861149.

The Ride

This two-day adventure from the seaport of Whitehaven to Cockermouth takes advantage of a cycleway which runs into the foothills of the Western fells where there is an obligatory detour to the shores of the remote but beautiful Ennerdale Water. The route climbs to a summit above Loweswater and detours to the very northern tip of Crummock Water before heading for Cockermouth. The return is by way of quiet villages in the lesser known area lying between Eaglesfield and Whitehaven.

Seeing Places

Cockermouth: Situated at the confluence of the Rivers Cocker and Derwent this pleasantly located town is the birthplace of poet William Wordsworth in 1770. The house now in National Trust hands is open to the public.

Whitehaven: Often referred to as the 'Georgian Port' because of its central core of 18th century housing, Whitehaven is a bustling centre. Its harbour is a major feature and has now been designated as a conservation area and a little fishing fleet still survives from this base. The story of the towns' development is told in the nearby museum.

Wythop: A mill complex restored to working order in the recent past, now open to the public.

Ennerdale (Copeland District Council)

The Route

1. The first leg of the journey is on the Whitehaven to Ennerdale cyclepath into the Cumbrian hills. The first section is a preliminary route but during the next year or so a permanent signed route will be established on the ground thus rendering this description defunct. In the meantime, be careful as you are mixing with Whitehaven's traffic. On leaving Whitehaven railway station, turn right (after 70 metres) through the supermarket car park towards the quayside. Cross over the road and follow the path for 50 metres leading to the quayside. Follow the quayside until you reach Harbour Square.

2. Turn left towards Golden Lion House. Cross the main road into the market place. Keep ahead as far as the Fitness Centre where you turn left into Queen Street where you will have to wheel your bike against the flow of traffic. Turn right into Cross Street, then turn right into Irish Street and first left into Howgill Street. Once agin, dismount here to walk against the flow on a one-way street. Pass the Timber Centre and go straight on into Richmond Terrace.

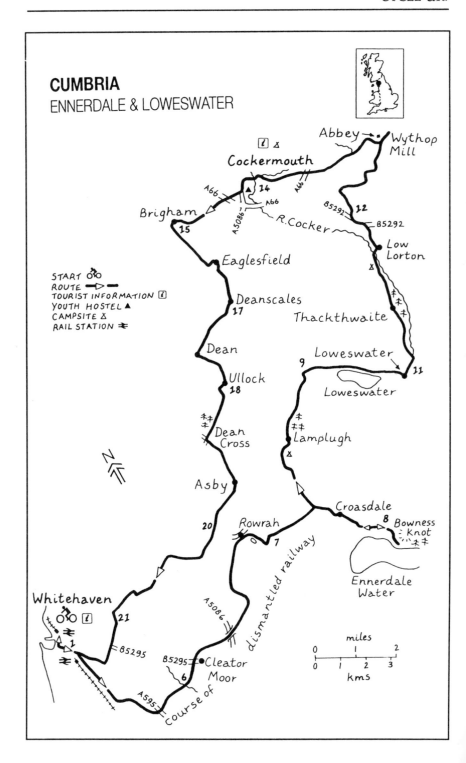

CUMBRIA
ENNERDALE & LOWESWATER

Abbey — Wythop Mill

Cockermouth

Brigham

14

15

Eaglesfield

R.Cocker

B5292 12

B5292

Low Lorton

START
ROUTE
TOURIST INFORMATION ℹ
YOUTH HOSTEL ▲
CAMPSITE ⌂
RAIL STATION ⇌

Deanscales
17

Thackthwaite

Dean

Ullock
18

Loweswater
9

Loweswater

11

Dean Cross

Lamplugh

Asby

Croasdale

Rowrah

20

7

Bowness Knot
8

Ennerdale Water

Whitehaven

21

A5086

dismantled railway

Course of

B5295

1

Cleator Moor

B5295

6

A595

miles
0   1   2
0   1   2   3
kms

3. On reaching Whitehaven Rugby Union Football Club follow the path to the right-hand side of the building and continue on the path until you reach the railway line on your right-hand side. Follow the railway line until you reach Coach Road. Cross over diagonally right and follow a made-up lane along the opposite side of the railway line, passing a football field, Whitehaven Rugby League Football Club and Athletic Ground.

4. After 500 metres the footpath turns left underneath the railway (beware of the low headroom) coming out onto Esk Avenue. Turn right and proceed for 300 metres. Turn right just before St Gregory's and St Patrick's Roman Catholic School and follow the cycleway through Pow Valley Meadows. After 600 metres turn right beneath the railway and then immediately left following the line of the beck, crossing over three bridges before arriving at Newlands Avenue.

5. Continue for 200 metres then turn left through open ground onto Wasdale Close. Continue for 100 metres and turn left under the railway and then immediately right onto the cycleway. Follow it towards a concrete road bridge for 350 metres. Proceed ahead under the left-hand bay of the road bridge at Cleator Moor.

6. It then runs through the urban areas of Mirehouse and Cleator Moor. It begins to level more as it passes to the west of Frizington and through the outskirts of Rowrah. From here the cycle path narrows and rises to join a narrow country lane. Go left to the junction by the school and turn right to ride up to Kirkland.

7. Keep ahead at the crossroads at Kirkland and climb once again to an isolated junction. Turn right for the steep drop into Croasdale and to a junction at Whins. Continue ahead for Ennerdale, with spectacular views. The road reaches Bowness Knott where there is a car park. Those seeking overnight accommodation at Ennerdale Youth Hostel should follow the waterside route through to Gillerthwaite.

8. Retrace your route to Croasdale and take the right turn for Felldyke, something of a climb for the best part of this section. A more level road winds through to Lamplugh, ignoring two turns to the left. Pass by the impressive gates to Lamplugh Hall and keep ahead at the junction making your way to towards Fangs Brow Farm, images of vampires in your mind as you back-pedal.

9. The road descends to a junction to the left of the farm. There is an option here for those seeking an off-road detour. Go left for Mockerkin where you turn right and right again in the village for Mosser. This narrow route climbs and dips through the farmstead of Sosgill to Mosser Mains where a group of tracks gather. Your way is first

right before the conglomerate to climb ferociously up through the farms at Mossergate. The track, which is heralded as unfit for cars rises up the shoulders of Mosser Fell before descending in earnest to the wooded waterside of Loweswater.

10. Others staying on the country lanes route should turn right at Fangs Brow to ride down to Waterend where lunch may be taken or eggs and other farm products purchased at Waterend Farm. Ride on by the quiet waters of Loweswater. There's a little climbing to do at the southern end towards the hamlet of Loweswater itself. Turn right for the Kirkstile Inn and Loweswater church. The road bends left to rejoin the main route.

11. Go right to rejoin the road to cross the River Cocker and, once over the bridge, go right again for a waterside wander alongside the upper edges of Crummock Water. Retrace your steps to the bridge and once over go right to ascend a little lane to a junction. Turn right and follow this lovely route through Latterhead farmstead and the cottages of Thackwaite to a junction at Low Lorton. Go right to cross the Cocker again and soon reach another junction by Lorton Hall. Turn left here if you want to pass the Wheatsheaf public house for refreshment on the B5289 towards Cockermouth. Diversionists can cross over to take the road towards High Lorton but turning next left to pass by Lorton church before re joining the main road at a bend.

12. The B5292 soon joins and you ride on to Cockermouth. There is soon a pleasant option if you wish but please do not take this right turn lightly as this is a busy route at times. Go right along a narrow lane to climb to Armaside Farm. Ignore the next turning right but then take the one after to Jenkin and High Side, a little known road running along the shoulders of Long and Ling Fell. It dips down to Tom Rudd Beck and a junction. Go right here and straight on at the next junction. Take the left fork and hold your brakes for a sharp descent to Wythop Mill.

13. Retrace your route back up the hillside and bear right and right again to descend into the valley. The lane winds its way to join a wider road coming in from Lambfoot. Keep ahead and at the crossroads turn right onto the B5292 into Cockermouth, a possible overnight stop.

14. From Cockermouth take the A594 out of town. It bends right and then rises along Lamplugh Road. Look for the third turning on the right into the old Brigham Road. Follow this to the very end where a small link path cuts through a hedge to the A66 Cockermouth by pass. Cross with caution as cars speed along here. Join the Brigham road, a wide and sometimes busy route up to the village.

15. By the Apple Tree public house turn left and left again on the road which climbs and climbs up to a quarry (close your eyes and ears) and then dips to Eaglesfield. Turn left into the village. The road bends right and on the corner is the birthplace of the famous physicist, John Dalton, at Dalton House. Turn next right and right again in the village. Then go left for the back lane to Deanscales.

16. If you are looking for an off-road alternative, go first right on the road out of Eaglesfield and this high-sided track runs between fields to the Dean Road. If not keep ahead and at the next fork bear right for the run into Deanscales.

17. In Deanscales, turn right to join the road to Dean. The off-road route rejoins this just before a climb. At the head of this there's another track off to the left which is a little off-road cut through to the village. Otherwise, continue to the crossroads where you bear left and come to the next junction in Dean itself (where the off-road enters). If you fancy an earlier lunch there's a fine pub a few metres ahead and on the right, the Royal Yew.

18. If pressing on, turn right to run along a sweet lane to Ullock. The last drop brings you to a car park and seats by the waters of the youthful River Marron.

19. Turn right here to cross the river and then take the next left for the climb and possibly walk up to Dean Cross. Turn left at crossroads for a welcome descent to Wright Green where you follow the bend of the road right before climbing again to Asby. Turn right here and right again at the end of the village to Arlecdon.

20. You'll know you have arrived at the northern eastern end of the village when you ride by the traditional Sun Inn, another possible lunchtime stop - for it is an hour's ride into Whitehaven now. At the junction, keep ahead along a narrower road through rough land. Turn right at the next junction to ease down to the Dub Beck before the hard climb up Weddicar Rigg, keeping left at the T-junction.

21. This signals the end of countryside riding for a while, for the road skirts an old open-cast mining area which is now the subject of an infill site. The road continues to a junction at Morseby Parks. Turn left and then straight on at the roundabout.

22. It's 'action alert' here, as you have now returned to the world of town traffic. Join the B5296 road down the hill at Hensingham which is busy. This drops down to traffic signals at a junction. Go right with the flow of the traffic but then ease up and dismount just before the Lowther Arms on the left where you cross the road.

23. Cycle along the short stretch of cycle route (the old main road) to the pedestrian lights. Cross over and go left into town down the Corcickle road, which is quite steep - so hold back because it is a busy thoroughfare. Follow the one way system down to the harbour; buy that well-earned ice cream and sit and watch the boats, if there are any, or seagulls which of there are bound to be hundreds by the time you're into your third lick.

GREAT CYCLING IDEAS!

The following list should be supplemented with the many bridleways used for off-road cycling, but take local advice as it is a sensitive issue!

Cumbria Cycleway: Mainly following the back roads of Cumbria this 250 miles plus circular route is well-liked by cyclists. A large fold out route description is available. Tel: Cumbria County Council (01539) 721000. Price: about £2.

Grizedale Forest Park: Several off-road routes are available at this superb venue.

Keswick Railway path to Threlkeld: four miles of off-road cycling in this very popular area.

Sea to Sea Cycle Route: a brilliant but sometimes hard 140 mile route developed by Sustrans from Workington or Whitehaven to Sunderland and Newcastle. Booklet available.

Also available is a leaflet *Cycling From The Cyclepath* from Groundwork in West Cumbria.

Talkin Tarn: Mountain bike routes leaflet is available at this water based country park near Brampton for a small charge.

Cycle Holiday Companies

*Eden Cycle Tours and Holidays,*Unit 8, Redhills, Penrith, CA11 0DL. Tel: (01768) 864884; *Not Just a Bike Shop,* Lake Road, Bowness-on-Windermere, LA23 3BJ. Open: all year. Also cycle hire.

Pedals & Boots, Cobblestones, Haverthwaite, Ulverston, LA12 8JW. Superb breaks on offer. Tel: (01539) 531391.

Wilderness on Wheels, Southey Hill, Keswick, Cumbria, CA5 1EA. Open: Easter to September for holidays. Cycle hire all year. Tel: (01768) 775202.

Long Meg and Her Daughters (Eden Tourism)

Cycle Hire Companies

Ambleside: *Ambleside Mountain Bikes*, c/o Scotts café, Waterhead, LA22 0EY. Open: March to October but other months by arrangement. Tel: (01539) 432014 or 434853; *Stuart Cunningham Outdoor Centres*, 1-2 Rydal Road, LA22 9AN. Open: all year. Tel: (01539) 432636.

Bowness-on-Windermere: *Daisy Cycle Hire*, Ashley House, 135 Craig Walk. Open: all year. Tel: (01539) 442144.

Brampton: *Talkin Tarn Country Park Cycle Hire*, CA8 1HN. Open: Easter to October. Tel: (01697) 73129.

Coniston: *Summitreks*, 14 Yewdale Road, LA21 8DU. Open: all year. Tel: (01539) 441212. Run exciting daily activity programmes.

Frizington: *Track and Trail*, Beech House, Frizington, CA26 3TH. Open: all year. Tel: (01946) 861149.

Grizedale: *Grizedale Mountain Bikes*, Old Hall Car Park, Grizedale Forest Centre, Near Hawkshead, LA22 OQJ. Open: March to November. Tel: (01229) 860369.

Hawkshead: *The Croft Mountain Bike Centre*, Charlotte Barn, North Lonsdale Rd, LA22 0NX. Open: All Year. Tel: (01539) 436374.

Kendal: *Askew Cycles*, Kent Works, Burneside Road, LA9 4RL. Open: all year. Tel: (01539) 728057.

Keswick: *Braithwaite General Stores*, near Keswick, CA12 5ST. Open: all year. Tel: (01768) 778273; *Keswick Motor Company*, Lake Road, CA12 5BX. Open: all year. Tel: (01768) 772064; *Ridgeway Mountain Bikes*, Visitor Centre, Whinlatter Forest Park, near Keswick. Open: all year. Tel: (01768) 778023 or mobile 'phone (0836) 331564.

Kirkby Stephen: *H.S. Robinson*, 2 Market Street, CA17 4QS. BR. Open: all year. Tel: (01768) 371519.

Ulverston: *South Lakeland Cycles*, Mill Farm, Lowick Bridge, near Ulverston, LA12 8EF. Open: all year. Tel: (01229) 885210.

Sedbergh: *Cobble Country Holidays*, 63 Main Street, Sedbergh, LA10 5AB. Open: all year. Tel: (01539) 621000.

Windermere: *Pleasure in Leisure*, Tirobeck, Keldwyth Park, LA23 1HG. Open: all year. Tel: (01539) 442324. Guided tours also available.

NORTHUMBRIA

Including Cleveland, Durham, Northumberland,
Tyne and Wear
Tourist Information: Northumbria Tourist Board,
Aykley Heads, Durham DH1 5UY. Tel: 0191 375 3000

The Kingdom of Northumbria has always been remote, as it is today. Beyond the urban coastal strip of Cleveland and Tyne and Wear, you will find that the magnificent North Eastern countryside is largely yours. Ride out to the Cleveland hills or through Teesdale and there is a freshness about the landscape. In many respects the upper haunts of Teesdale and Weardale are very unspoilt. These surrounding hills were at one time threaded by lead mines but they are now as wild and isolated as in the centuries before the mining boom 150 years ago. A combination of high hills and harsh winters have combined to thwart the scattered farmsteads hereabouts but it is certainly a landscape to inspire the hardy cyclist.

County Durham must surely be one of the premier spots for making good use of old disused railways to bridge the gap between town and country. There are several rides from the cathedral city of Durham itself, which was a formidable seat of power in the land of the Prince Bishops. The ride from Sunderland to Consett is essential for those who enjoy sculpture at its best, for Sustrans has excelled itself on this trail which leads to the award-winning Beamish Museum and the shoulders of the North Pennines, a real wilderness. There are also great rides along the banks of the Tyne and through the Derwent Valley.

Hadrian's Wall is no divider now but the borderland north of it is little populated, probably because of the fear of bloody skirmishes in past centuries. There are several brilliant rides through forested areas and the cycling centre of Northumbria, Kielder, where there are off-road routes galore around the extensive waters of Kielder reservoir. Not that the Northumberland coast should be ignored, for there are fine beaches and sturdy castles, as at Bamburgh. There are also the little coastal villages of Seahouses, Craster and Alnmouth which grew up as fishing ports and still retain that air of the sea.

COUNTRYSIDE RIDE

Wilderness Wheeling in Weardale

A mountain bike adventure described by Katy and Ian Perrin of Weardale Mountain Bikes.

Distance: 40 miles.

Terrain: Strenuous. Suitable for mountain bikes only.

Map: O.S. Landranger 92 or Outdoor Leisure Map 31.

Rail Access: Nearest railhead is Bishop Auckland.

Accommodation and Refreshment: The Moorcock Inn at Eggleston offers refreshment and accommodation. Other bed and breakfast establishments are in the village and in nearby Romaldkirk. Tourist Information is available at Barnard Castle. Tel: (01833) 690909.

Cycle Hire: Weardale Mountain Bikes.

The Ride

The North Pennines have been described as "England's Last Wilderness". This little known area, lying between the Yorkshire Dales and Scottish borders, is now rightly designated as an Area of Outstanding Natural Beauty. There is no better way of discovering its beauty than by bike.

Frosterley is the starting point for this varied partly off-road tour, which could be completed by a hardened mountain biker in a day or conveniently spread over two days for lesser mortals! There are plenty of climbs and even more wilderness, so take good advice before setting off.

Seeing Places

Frosterley: Frosterley lies in the heart of Weardale, a mile or two along the valley from the larger settlement of Stanhope. The entire area was once famous for its lead mining and the Killhope Lead Mining Centre on the A689 road to Alston is a superbly restored lead mining site standing beneath the impressive 34-feet high water wheel.

Frosterley is better known for its quarrying of marble and the stone has been used for ornamental purposes in several churches in County Durham including Durham Cathedral.

Hamsterley Forest: This extensive forest, estimated to be over 2500 hectares in size, has been opened up for leisure, including the use of forestry tracks for cycling. There is a visitor centre near to the entrance off the Hamsterley Road which depicts the working life of the forest.

The Route

1. From the Weardale Mountain Bike Centre turn right on the main A689 road and then bear next left at the corner onto the B5278 signposted to Eggleston. Cross the bridge over the River Wear, go through the quiet quarter known as Bridge End and begin to climb out of the valley.

2. As the road bends sharp right turn left onto a narrow lane to White Kirkley, now joining the Weardale Way. It dips to a tributary of the Wear and then climbs as a gated road to the fells. You reach an impressive stone building called Allotment House, a solitary family dwelling in previous decades. It must have been a tough existence at this bleak and lonely place.

3. The road surface ends and the final section to the fell top at 380 metres is a challenging climb. Turn left along the moorland track with stunning views of Weardale to the north and heather covered grouse moors stretching away to the south. When the track eventually meets tarmac turn right to ride southwards. This rises up and dips to cross the Harthope Beck before eventually giving out onto moorland beyond Blackburn Lodge at a gate.

4. The ride now takes you across open moorland. At the next stone wall you go through Doctor's Gate, a reference no doubt to an earlier incident. Fork left and follow the track across moorland until it bends left; turn right onto a smaller track which you follow carefully until a gate is reached into Hamsterley Forest (Grid Ref. 072316).

5. Proceed to the track ahead (a fire break) and follow it right. This leads to a ford across the Ayhope Beck and then climbs the far bank in a civilised fashion. Stay on this main track through several intersections and you will be rewarded with a fine downhill run which curves left and then straight to the Euden Beck.

6. When you reach the intersection with the valley track (Grid Reference 058301) go sharp left to go to The Grove, a large house in the

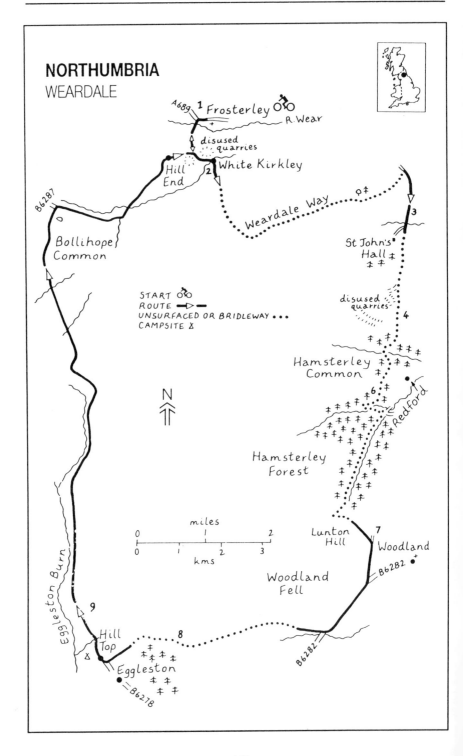

centre of the forest. Join the road and go right, then right again to follow the Forest Drive along the Spurlswood Beck. This comes to a car park entrance at Lunton Hill but you cross the bridge to climb the hillside out of Hamsterley Wood.

7. Go right at the junction and right again at the B6282. Continue on this road for approximately half a mile passing Hindon Farm and Dale Terrace. As the road dips to Hindon Beck, go right along a narrow lane to the appropriately named Woolly Hill Farm.

8. The bridleway crosses Woodland Fell where there are magnificent views over Teesdale. The route runs to the edge of Stobgreen Plantation and then by a house to a straight descent to Hill Top, near Eggleston, in Teesdale.

9. The return route follows the B6278 (by turning right) which, in places, crosses the old Roman road along the shoulders of Eggleston Common and Islington Hill.

10. The road climbs Low Black Hill and crosses Bollihope Common. Look for a turning to Bollihope and Frosterley on your right.

11. Return by way of Hill End, a name which strikes anguish into many road cyclists' hearts, but this is just a steady climb in reality. The descent to Frosterley provides a fitting climax to what can only be described as an exhilarating route.

GREAT CYCLING IDEAS!

Cycling as a recreational activity is being encouraged in Northumbria. The opportunities to escape into numerous backwaters makes it a very attractive proposition for a cycling holiday. There are miles of country lanes where you can simply ride away from it all.

Cleveland

Cycle Rides in Cleveland: Three road routes of 16 to 28 miles in duration to local places of interest such as Guisborough and Staithes. Leaflet available. Small charge.

Middlesbrough Cycleways: a leaflet describing approved routes in Middlesbrough. Useful for escaping into the countryside.

Durham Cathedral (Durham County Council)

County Durham

Consett and Sunderland Railway Path: This 16-mile Sustrans path links coast and hills and provides access to the Beamish Museum. This is very much a sculpture trail! Leaflet available. Now forms part of C2C route.

Countryside Cycling, Teesdale and Richmondshire: three routes specifically designed for family cycling in Teesdale, one of the Durham dales in the Land of the Prince Bishops. Leaflet available. Small charge.

Cycling in County Durham: a beautifully presented pack suggesting five routes in the county (Low Pittington, Beamish, Brandon, Neasham and Hurworth, Lanchester and Deerness) with additional information on cycling. Price range: £1 - £2. Tel: County Durham 0191 386 4411.

Haswell to Hart Countryside Walkway: nine miles of off-road path in East Durham. Leaflet available. Small charge.

Railway Walks in Derwentside: four leaflets covering railway paths mentioned elsewhere.

Railway Walks in County Durham: a pack of 6 route cards explaining these attractive railpath routes: Bishop Auckland to Spennymoor; Brandon to Bishop Auckland; Deerness Valley Walk; Derwent Walk; Lanchester Valley Walk; Waskerley Way, all 4-12 miles. Price: £2-£3.

Northumberland

Border Forest Park Guide Map and Routes: several routes in this borderland mainly under forest. Price range: £1 - £2. Contact Kielder Bikes (01434) 220932.

Cycle Routes from Tower Knowe Visitor Centre, Kielder: leaflet available. Small charge. Tel: (01434) 240398.

Cycling in North Northumberland: super pack of 5 cycle rides in a great cycling patch. Available from local tourist information offices. Charge.

Kielder Mountain Bike Routes: six mountain bike routes varying from moderately strenuous to tough. Forest Enterprise is also introducing a 'Trail Quest' cyclo-orienteering area which sounds very impressive.

Tyne Riverside Country Park: along the Wylam Waggonway from Prudhoe to Wylam and Newburn. Five miles, off-road.

North Sea Cycleway: over 300 miles from Berwick on Tweed to the Humber. Contact New Riders of the Open Road, Laurieston Hall, Castle Douglas, Kirkcudbrightshire DG7 2NB.

Tyne and Wear

North Tyne Cycleway: runs for eight miles, with breaks, from the historic quarters of Newcastle Quayside to Newburn and Wylam.

South Tyne Cycleway: a route from Jarrow to Swalwell.

The Steel Bonnet: a 200 mile circular ride between youth hostels in Newcastle, Wooler and Greenhead. From Y.H.A.

Cycle Holiday Companies

By-Cycle, St Anthony's House, 14 Stakeford Lane, Stakeford, Choppington, Northumberland NE62 5JB. Open: last week of May to the first week of September. Tel: (01670) 813769. Self-guided holidays arranged.

Cheviot Hillbillies, Kypie Farm, Mindrum, Milfield, Wooler, TD12 4QG. Enterprising cycle holiday company who also offer cycle friendly accommodation. Tel: (01668) 216308.

Tandem Tours, Newbiggin Hill Farmhouse, Hexham, Northumberland NE46 1TA. Open: all year, but pre-booking preferred. Tel: (01434) 604209. Tandem riding through Northumbria sounds great fun.

Weardale Mountain Bikes, 39 Front Street, Frosterley near Stanhope, DL13 2QP. Open: all year, but closed on Tuesdays and Winter Sundays (Oct-Mar). Tel: (01388) 528129. Cycle Hire also available.

Cycle Hire Companies

Cleveland:

Darlington: *Tensor Marketing Ltd*, Lingfield Way, Yarm Road Industrial Estate, DL1 4XX. Open: all year. Tel: (01325) 469181. BR.

Great Ayton: *Bike Tech*, 39a High St. Open: All year. Tel: (01642) 724444.

Middlesbrough: *Colin Armstrong Cycles*, 22-24 Princes Road, Middlesbrough, TS1 4BB. Open: all year. Tel: (01642) 244027. BR.

Durham:

Consett: *Consett Bicycle Company*, 62-64 Medomsley Rd. Open: all year, need prior notice out of season. Tel: (01207) 581205; *Derek McVickers Sports*, 23 Front St, Consett, DH8 5AB. Open: all year. Tel: (01207) 505121.

Durham: *Dave Heron Cycles*, 6 Neville Street, DH1 4EY. BR. Open: all year. but prior notice required out of season. Tel: 0191 384 0287.

Hamsterley Forest: *Hamsterley Forest Bikes Hire Centre*, Hamsterley Forest. Open: long summer season. Tel: (01388) 528129.

Derwentside cycle path (Durham County Council)

Northumberland:

Amble: *Breeze Bikes,* Coquet Street, Open: All year. Tel: (01665) 710323.

Hexham: *Fewster's Shop,* 48 Priestpopple, NE46 1PP. Open: all year. Tel: (01434) 603511.

Kielder: *Kielder Bikes,* Hawhope Car Park, Kielder Water, NE48 1BX. Open: April to October, pre-booking required at other times. Tel: (01434) 250392; *Cyclery* at Castle Hill open all year (except Fridays out of season).

Warbottle: *Cheviot Bikes,* Low Alwinton, Warbottle, Morpeth, NE65 7BE. Open: all year. Tel: (01669) 50224. Self catering cottages available.

Wooler: *Kimmerston Riding Centre,* Milfield, NE71 6GH. Open: All Year. Tel: (01668) 216283; *Wooler Cycle Hire,* Padgepool Place, NE71 6BL. Tel: (01668) 281600.

Tyne & Wear:

Sunderland: *Darke Cycles,* St Thomas Street. Open: all year. Tel: 0191 510 8155. BR.

WALES

Includes Brecon Beacons and Snowdonia and the quiet tracks of Mid-Wales
Tourist Information: Wales Tourist Board, Brunel House, 2 Fitzalan Road, Cardiff CF2 1UY. Tel: (01222) 499909

The soft green pastures and hillsides of Wales, the high mountains of the North and the valleys of Mid- and South Wales are impressive to the visitor. An increasing proportion of this green land is protected, for there are three National Parks: the Brecon Beacons, Pembrokeshire and Snowdonia and others, such as the Llyn Peninsula, are designated as Areas of Outstanding Natural Beauty.

Much of the landscape, of course, is due to the fascinating geology of Wales with the oldest rocks forming the backbone from Snowdonia through the Cambrian Mountains to the Preseli hills in Pembrokeshire where mountain bikers now seek out the old drove roads with unmetalled surfaces. The rivers of Wales are another strong feature, for example, the vales of the Severn, Wye, Usk and Teifi. Wales is both wild and soft.

The problems for the cycle tourer are the gateway 'A' roads, which are packed with lorries and caravans jostling for a space in the queue. Some have suggested that the lack of motorway-style fast roads into Wales has slowed the development of tourism. Forbid the thought for major road building would ruin the very nature of Wales which attracts those who love the outdoors.

There are not many designed cycle routes here but there are miles and miles of unclassified roads which allow a freedom of spirit for the cyclist. This is the essence of Wales, and cycling here can bring immeasurable fun if you know where to go. Snowdonia is currently the main attractor and suffers from the pressures of numbers. Thus off-road cycling is restricted by a voluntary agreement but elsewhere recommended routes hold as much promise. This is especially true of the Brecon Beacons and the Marches. Cycle touring through the back roads of Dyfed, on the other hand, could not be a greener pastime.

The great news is that the Wales National Cycle Route is now being implemented and within the next 2-3 years it will be possible to cycle from Holyhead to Chepstow or Cardiff.

COUNTRYSIDE RIDE

An exhilarating Day Ride through the Brecon Beacons

Distance: 30 miles.

Terrain: Strenuous. Mountain Bike required.

Maps: O.S. Landranger maps 160 Brecon and 161 Abergavenny.

Rail Access: Nearest point is Abergavenny with daily bus to Talybont and Brecon.

Accommodation: Brecon and Talybont have accommodation and there is a youth hostel near Brecon. There is no refreshment point until Talybont on the route but a shop and pubs are available here, Pencelli and Llanfrynach. Tel: Tourist Information (01874) 622485.

Cycle Hire: there is cycle hire at Brecon and the Talybont Venture Centre in Talybont.

The Ride

This is not an easy ride. There is a hefty climb up to the gap between the summits of Cribyn and Fan y Big, on this ancient way thought to be an old Roman Road. First there is a steep road climb out of Brecon and then a track route up which climbs the shoulders of Cwm Cynwyn. Get these behind you and the rest is plain sailing and for the most part downhill.

You join the Taff Trail for a journey back to Brecon with a seven-mile descent to Talybont village before returning to Brecon along back lanes.

Seeing Places

Brecon: is an old-established market town made famous by its international jazz festival. It also serves as a tourist centre and gateway for those seeking outdoor activities. The Brecon Beacons are a range of impressive mountains, many of which are over 2000ft and Pen-y-Fan rises to 2,907ft. The views are brilliant but make sure that you are wearing the right clothing, for it is easy to become chilled on the tops.

Talybont-on-Usk: You pass by Talybont reservoir on your descent to Talybont village. Built in the 1930s the reservoir supplies Newport with drinking water. It is designated as a Site of Special Scientific Interest and attracts a wide range of wintering birds. Talybont village lies on a crossroads of the Monmouthshire and Brecon canal and the old Merthyr to Brecon railway, as well as several roads. The Star pub in the village is well-known for its vast selection of real ales and jazz nights.

Cycling through Talybont-on-Usk (Chris Rushton)

The Route

1. From Brecon town centre, turn left to leave on the main road to Senybridge, crossing over the River Usk. Pass Brecon College on the left. Take a left turn after the garage signposted to Llanfaes.

2. Cross the small roundabout and begin to climb with the hospital to your right. The climbing really begins in earnest at Baileyhelig and then descends to a junction where Taff Trail signs can be seen.

3. Keep ahead here, gaining a respite after that hard pedalling. The promise of the mountains is signalled by the bold outlines of the scarp edges of the Beacons. Ignore turnings to the left and right but at the coming T-junction go right. There are no signposts.

4. This narrow road dips down to a stream and then rises up sharply to a stony lane, often with a car or two parked at its entrance. You soon reach a gate which opens out into a large pasture.

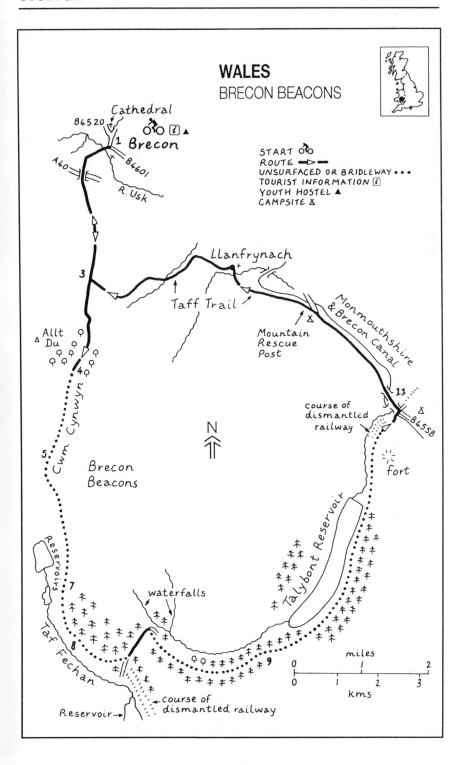

WALES
BRECON BEACONS

Cathedral
B4520
1 Brecon
A40
B4601
R. Usk

START ♂
ROUTE ➡▬
UNSURFACED OR BRIDLEWAY •••
TOURIST INFORMATION Ⓘ
YOUTH HOSTEL ▲
CAMPSITE ⊿

Llanfrynach
3
Taff Trail
Mountain
Rescue
Post
Monmouthshire & Brecon Canal

Allt Du
4
Cwm Cynwyn
5
Brecon Beacons

course of
dismantled
railway
11
B4558
fort

N

Reservoirs
7
waterfalls
Talybont Reservoir

Taf Fechan
8
9

miles
0   1   2
0   1   2   3
kms

Reservoir→
course of
dismantled railway

5. Follow the clear track along the valley side with exceptional views across the Beacons. The track is strewn with rocks and very often pitted with pools and trickling springs. The last climb up to the gap is exhilarating, but few manage to ride this last steep section.

6. Pause to admire the panorama. The chances are you will not be alone here for it is a well-known crossing of paths and an increasingly popular high-level cycle ride. The track descends gently with views across to Neaudd Reservoir.

7. You come to a triangular junction. Your way is to the left into a gully and up a very steep bank to a bridleway which skirts the wood to join a road. You will have to dismount to tackle the gully. Some avoid it by bearing right at the junction and then down a track to a gate. They cut left just before to cross a stile and join a single road near to the buildings.

8. Either way you will soon meet the Taff Trail. Go left along a green track. This becomes a forestry route which leads to the metalled road from Talybont to Ponsticill. This is not too busy except on Summer Sunday afternoons. Go left to climb up to the summit and, as the road begins to wind its way down into the valley, go right onto the forestry track as signposted.

9. The rest is bliss, nearly seven miles of downhill sections through woodland. Hold back as you pass an opening where the top end of the reservoir can be seen, for this about the best view you'll get because of the tree cover lower down.

10. You will see the dam on the left. By all means, make a detour for a view across the water. Your route eases up a bank to a junction, then joins a rougher descent into Talybont entering by way of a bridge over the Monmouth and Brecon Canal.

11. In Talybont, go left and follow the Taff Trail waymarks to Pencelli, Llanfrynach and onward to Brecon.

GREAT CYCLING IDEAS!

Clwyd

Cycle Clwyd: booklet describing 14 circular rides. Information available on (01352) 702870.

Glyndwr Cycle Routes: through the wilder parts of Clwyd - the old haunts of Wales's most famous warriors. Leaflet available.

Dyfed

Circular Routes in the Pembrokeshire National Park: Leaflet available to describe leafy lane and coastal rides.

Mid-Glamorgan

Parc Cwm Darran Cycleway: A rail path from Bargoed to Pentwyn. 3.5 miles on an old railway trackbed.

The Taff Trail: a great route from Cardiff to Brecon, following the trackways of the Valleys to the forested tops of the Beacons. Route booklet available. Small charge.

South Glamorgan

Penarth to Sully Cycle Route: a short run between these seaside towns. Leaflet available.

The Taff Trail: see the listing under Mid Glamorgan for details.

West Glamorgan

Afan Valley Cycleways: Routes in the forested Afan Valley based on the Afan Argoed Country Park. Leaflet available.

Swansea Bikepath: a seaside route from the Swansea Maritime Quarter to Mumbles. About 5 miles but there is also a link to the Clyne Valley.

Gwent

The Newport to Abergavenny Leisure Route: sections are available from Malpas to Cwmbran, Cwmbran to Pontypool and Talywain. When developed this will be a superb run through Gwent eastern fringe.

Sirhowy Valley Railpath: there is a 5-mile section of path from Gelligoes to Newtown in a surprisingly beautiful valley.

Gwynedd

Coed-y-Brenin Forest Park Map: including mountain bike trails. Price range: £1 - £2. Mountain bike runs in rugged forestry north of Dolgellau.

Explorer: a guide to 20 cycling routes in and around Snowdonia. Price range: £7 - £8. Available from local Tourist Information Centres.

Gwydyr Forest: there are specially waymarked routes through the forest, permits required to ride on them. A Guide Map is available. Price range: £2 - £3. Tel: Llanrwst Forest District Office for details on (01492) 640578.

Lôn Eifion: a cycle-path from Caernarfon to Bryncir and then by minor roads to the seaside resort of Criccieth totalling 19 miles. The views across Caernarfon Bay and to the mountains of Snowdonia make the path all that more enjoyable.

Mawddach Walk: an 8 mile rail-path from Mawddach Railway station and Dolgellau via Penmaenpool. Ideal for bird-watching.

Snowdonia and its Coast Walks and Cycle Rides: booklet outlining four road cycle rides in the territory between Caernarfon and Bala.

Snowdonia Cyclists National Voluntary Cycling Agreement: leaflet available which is aimed at controlling the level of uses of the bridleways to Snowdon summit for off-road cycling - voluntary ban on off-road cycling on many bridleways between 10am and 5pm daily from mid-May until the end of September.

Powys

Kerry Ridgeway: a route along an ancient way from Cider House Farm to Bishops Castle in Shropshire. Wild country and pleasant riding on this 15-mile route. Leaflet available. Small charge.

Suggestions for Short Rides from Llandrindod Wells: leaflet describing five on-road rides from Llandrindod Wells to marvellous Radnorshire corners such as Alpine Bridge, Abbeycwmhir and Newbridge on Wye. Leaflet available. Small charge.

Cycle Holiday Companies

Beacons Experience, 2 Forest Lodge Cottages, Libanus, Brecon, LD3 8NW. Open: All year. Tel: (01874) 623177.

Bicycle Beano, Brynderwen, Erwood, Builth Wells, Powys, LD2 3PQ. Open: Easter, then May through to September. Tel: (01982) 560471. A very well-known company offering great tours and good cooking.

Berwyn Mountain Holidays, Nantlais, Quarry Road, Glyn Ceiriog, Llangollen, Clwyd LL20 7DA. Open: all year. Tel: (01691) 718845.

Brecon and Beyond, Blaen Cai, LD3 8YR. Open: All Year. Tel: (01874) 636484. CH also available.

Clive Powell Mountain Bikes, The Mount, East Street, Rhayader, LD6 5DN. Open: all year. Tel: (01597) 810585. Made "Dirty Weekends" famous in Mid-Wales.

Landsker Countryside Holidays, SPARC, The Old School, Station Road, Narberth, SA67 8DU. Tel: (01834) 860965.

Puffin Cycle Tours, Middle Walls, Penally, Tenby, Dyfed SA70 7PG. Open: all year. Tel: (01834) 843057. Lovely self-guided tours around the National Park and West Wales. BR.

Red Kite Mountain Bike Centre, Neuadd Arms Hotel, Llanwrtyd Wells, Powys LD5 4RB. Open: all year. Tel: (01591) 3236. The home of bog snorkling, the Man versus Horse versus Bike race and Mid-Wales annual beer festival. Great mountain bike territory, good fun and beer. BR.

Tidevane Ltd, St Brides Hill, Saundersfoot, Dyfed SA69 9NH. Open: all year. Tel: (01834) 812304. Tours available in West and Mid-Wales. BR.

Mountain biking, Rhayader, Elan Valley (Chris Rushton)

Cycle Hire Companies

South Wales:

Dyfed (south)

Carmarthen: *Ar Dy Feic*, 20B Heol-y-Brenin, SA31. Open: All year. Tel: (01267) 221182. Also holidays available.

Haverfordwest: *Mikes Bikes*, 17 Prendergast, SA61 2PE. Open: All Year. Tel: (01437) 760068.

Mathry: *Preseli Mountain Bikes*, Parcynole Fach, near Haverfordwest SA62 5HN. Open: all year. Tel: (01348) 837709. Also activity centre, plus cottage for hire.

Newport: *Gwaun Valley Mountain Bikes*, Tyriet Cilgwyn near Newport, SA42 0QW. Open: all year. Tel: (01239) 820905.

South Glamorgan

Cardiff: *Taff Trail Cycle Hire*, Forest Farm Country Park, Whitchurch, CF4 7JH. Open: March to October. Tel: (01222) 822940. BR (Radyr).

West Glamorgan

Afan Argoed: *Afan Argoed Countryside Centre*, Afan Forest Park, Cynonville, near Port Talbot, SA13 3HG. Open: April to Sept. and weekends from November to March, but please check. Tel: (01639) 850564.

Swansea: *Clyne Valley Cycles*, 9 Walters Row, Dunvant, SA2 7TB. BR. Open: April to October. Tel: (01792) 208889. BR; *Swansea Bay Cycle Hire*, Village Lane, Boat Park, Mumbles. Open: All year. Tel (01792) 818248.

Gwent

Chepstow: *Bikeways*, 9 Wyebank Close, Wyebank Estate, NP6 7ET. Open: all year. Tel: (01291) 620932. Specialises in mountain bike rides and training. Groups only. BR.

Mid Wales:

Dyfed (Ceredigion)

Cilcennin: *Cyclemart*, Cilcennin, near New Quay. Open: Summer only. Tel: (01570) 470079.

Powys

Builth Wells: *Builth Wells Cycles*, Fairleigh, LD2 3AN. Open: All year. Tel: (01982) 551110.

Llandrindod Wells: *Greenstiles*, High Street, LD1 6AX. Open: all year. Tel: (01597) 824594. BR.

Llangedwyn: *Swallow Tandems*, Llangedwyn Mill. Also outlet at Lake Vrynwy. Tel: (01691) 780050. Organise great tandem events.

Llangorse: *Llangorse Lake Hire*, Llangorse, Brecon. Open: Main season. Tel: (01874) 84226.

Llanwddyn: Bethania Adventure, Cwm Cownwy, SY10 0NJ. Open: All year. Near Lake Vyrnwy.

Machynlleth: *Greenstiles*, 7 Hoel Penrallt, SY20 8AX. Open: all year. Tel: (01654) 703543. BR.

Talybont-on-Usk: *Talybont Venture Centre*, The Old Shop, LD3 7JD. Open: all year. Tel: (01874) 87458.

North Wales:

Clwyd

Llangollen: *Llansports*, 10 Berwyn Street, LL20 8ND. Open: all year. Tel: (01978) 860605.

Gwynedd

Beddgelert: *Beics Beddgelert,*Beddgelert Forest, LL55 4UU. Open: all year. Tel: (01766) 686434.

Betws-y-Coed: *Beics Betws*, LL24 0AU. Open: all year. Tel: (01690) 710766

Brynteg: *Tyddyn Philip Activity Centre*, Anglesey, LL78 8JF. Open: all year. Tel: (01248) 853439. Outdoor pursuits and multi activity courses.

Pwllheli: *Llyn Cycle Centre*, Lower Ala Road, LL53 5BU. Open: April to October. Tel: (01785) 612414. BR.

SCOTLAND

Includes both mainland Scotland and its islands
Tourist Information: Scottish Tourist Board,
23 Ravelston Terrace, Edinburgh, EH4 3HU.
Tel: 0131 332 2433

Scotland is breathtaking. The grandeur of the high mountains is matched only by the deepest lochs. Visitors are attracted to the national park areas of Ben Nevis and Glencoe, the Cairngorms and the wild glens of Affric, Cannich and Strathfarrar, the Trossachs and the Torridon Mountains. They undeniably make up the high ground of the UK where climber pits his or her wits against the elements. On the lower shoulders and in the valleys cyclists share this challenge with gusto.

There is also a romantic appeal about the Western and Hebridean islands where hardy settlers live through both the storm and calm of the Atlantic. Combining island hops with cycle rides is becoming fashionable again; trips to Arran, Isla and Jura, Harris and Skye, many of which have cycle hire available.

But Scotland is far more than this. Each region has its own distinction and opportunities for cycling off the beaten track. The Borders are underestimated as a destination and so is Dumfries and Galloway where you can follow in the footsteps of national poet Robbie Burns. Cycling out of the major cities of Glasgow and Edinburgh is also possible with over a 100 miles of railpath routes built in recent years. The regions of Central, Fife and Tayside, the central zone of Scotland also offers great cycling breaks around places like Aberfeldy, East Neuk and Dunkeld.

Grampian and the Highlands are firm favourites. Though vast in area, routes through these regions can be very busy with traffic in summer and the midges can become even more irksome. Cycle to Balmoral (the summer residence of the Royal Family) near Ballater, alongside the Findhorn or to Speyside, where mountain biking is very popular.

In the Highlands, the appeal of Ullapool, Gairloch and out-of-the-way places such as the Applecross peninsula entice the cycle tourer farther north, often in a classic Highlands and Islands tour. Some head by train (when space is available) to Thurso and take the ferry to Orkney or Shetland.

Scotland is undoubtedly the fastest growing cycle holiday and hire country in the United Kingdom. More routes are being devised for cycle touring throughout and there is a general feeling of enthusiasm and welcome for the cyclist. Put Scotland on your list.

Cycling in The Highlands (Scottish Tourist Board)

COUNTRYSIDE RIDE

Dumfries

Distance: 60 miles.

Terrain: Moderately strenuous. Suitable for touring cycles or ATBs.

Map: O.S. Landranger 84 Dumfries.

Rail Access: Dumfries.

Accommodation and Refreshment: There is ample accommodation in Dumfries and Castle Douglas as well as in the villages on the route. There is a youth hostel at Dumfries.

Cycle Hire: in Dumfries and Castle Douglas. See listing.

The Ride

Dumfries and Galloway has gone out of its way to make cyclists feel at home including a Welcome Scheme at local accommodation providers and attractions. Quite appropriate too for Nithsdale is the home of the pedal cycle and the KM Trail (mentioned below) heads for the birthplace, a pilgrimage that many a cyclist has made in recent years.

The ride follows several of the back roads of Dumfries to historic sites and the bustling town of Castle Douglas, which is a good spot for an overnight stop. It is a hilly route but there are very few severe climbs. It is an unpretentious landscape with few farms and hamlets where you'll see cottages in the vernacular white or pink wash. The return to Sweetheart Abbey is not as demanding and there should be plenty of time left in day two to spend the afternoon here or perhaps diverting to nearby Mabie Woods for a spot of mountain biking.

Seeing Places

Dumfries: Dumfries is all that one would expect from a regional capital standing above the banks of the Nith. Its association with the famous poet, Robbie Burns is well documented and at the top end of High Street there is a proud statue of the man himself, built as a tribute to his poetic genius in 1882. The following is inscribed on the statue plinth:

"O Scotia! My Dear, My Native Soil
For Whom My Warmest Wish to
Heaven is Sent!
Ev'n then a wish (I mind its power).
A wish that to my latest hour
Shall strongly have my breast
That I for poor auld Scotland's sake
Some useful plan or book could make
or sing a sang at least."

Burns House is where he spent the last years of his life and the Robert Burns Centre tells the story of this literary soul who is buried in a mausoleum of St Michael's churchyard.

Castle Douglas: on the outskirts of the town is Threave Gardens and Threave Castle, one of the many fine stone towers which were built in these parts during the 13th to 16th centuries. You will need to ring for the ferryman to take you across to this sinister looking fortress.

Drumcoltrum Tower: the ride also passes Drumcoltrum Tower, another roofed tower-house standing next to an 18th century farm.

New Abbey: the ruins of the Cistercian enclave known as Sweetheart Abbey founded in memory of John Balliol by his wife. She was also buried in the abbey and legend says that the embalmed heart of her husband was placed in a casket by her - hence the name. Just along the road is the New Abbey Cornmill, a water-powered mill restored as a working museum and, up above the village on the hillside, is the Waterloo Monument commemorating the Battle of Waterloo.

Mabie Forest: there's mountain bike hire here in the summer and a number of trails to follow.

The Route

1. From the Tourist Information Centre, in Whitesands, turn left and left at the traffic lights across the appropriately named Traffic Bridge. Keep ahead at the first junction but then position yourself for a right turn into Terregles Road.

2. Ride out of town, turning left just beyond a garage but still on Terregles Road which heads for the hills through Terregles village, keeping ahead at all times. The road rises to the left through woodland then dairy pastures to the pink and white cottages which make up the hamlet of Shawhead.

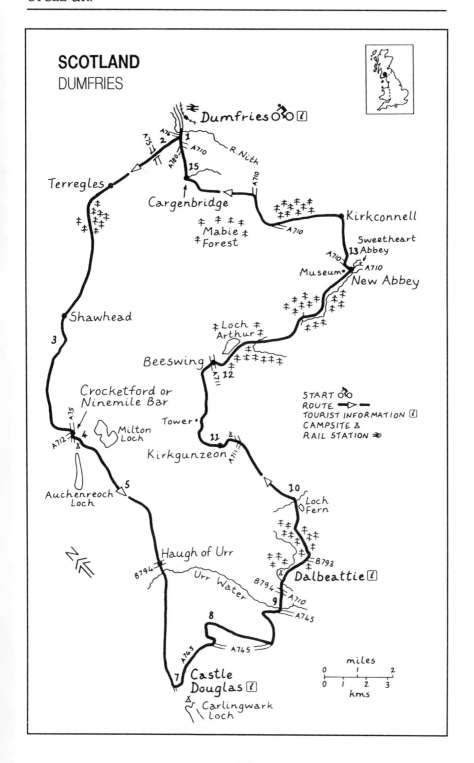

SCOTLAND
DUMFRIES

Dumfries

Terregles

Cargenbridge

Mabie Forest

Kirkconnell

Sweetheart Abbey

Museum

New Abbey

Shawhead

Loch Arthur

Beeswing

Crocketford or Ninemile Bar

Tower

Milton Loch

Kirkgunzeon

Auchenreoch Loch

Loch Fern

Haugh of Urr

Urr Water

Dalbeattie

Castle Douglas

Carlingwark Loch

START
ROUTE
TOURIST INFORMATION
CAMPSITE
RAIL STATION

miles
0   1   2
0   1   2   3
kms

161

3. Your road joins another and continues ahead, despite there being a left turn signposted to Castle Douglas. This narrow highway runs beneath Larglengee Hill to the main A75 at Crocketford, a good staging post for it has a garage, shop and the Galloway Arms.

4. Turn right onto the main road and shortly after the garage turn left along a lane signposted to Brandedleys Caravan Park which must be all but 100 metres up the bank. You'll catch a view of Auchenreoch Loch over the caravan roofs. Climb to a large farm and bear right here to climb the flanks of Tan Hill.

5. The lane reaches a summit and winds down to a junction with the old military road. Go right. The road rises to Hardgate and then drops sharply to a crossroads at Haugh of Urr. There's a post office on the left and the Laurie Arms a few paces along.

6. Go straight across the B794 down to a narrow bridge over the Urr Water. The road climbs to Blackerne then descends to the main road where a left turn is made for Castle Douglas. Follow the signs into the town centre along King Street. The tourist information centre is opposite the Crown Hotel in a car park.

7. Go through the car park to Queen Street. Turn left and then follow the A745 out of town towards Dalbeattie. Look for a turning one mile out (not a first turn left), on a large bend, signposted to Haugh. The lane bends left and rises alongside a deep sided stream bed. It bends right and straightens. Go next right up a narrow lane with a ridge of grass running along the centre.

8. This narrow lane rises relentlessly up to a farmstead and then by Dalbeattie reservoir before descending in earnest to the main road again. Turn left for a downhill spin, only to be stopped by traffic lights at the end of the narrow Buittle Bridge.

9. Turn left and ride along the A711 into Dalbeattie, a small town lying above the flood-plain of the Urr and the rising slopes of Dalbeattie Forest. Turn right in the town into High Street and then left into Alpine Street, right into Moss Road and then join the B793 to go left. Climb out of town and just when you have time to gain your strength go left to dip at first by a tip but then to climb remorselessly through the forest. This is the hardest section and walking is permitted, even lying down is permitted.

10. You eventually reach a T-junction, where you bear left along the road signposted to Kirkgunzeon. This soon descends along the slopes of the valley to the main A711 road. Turn right and first left. Keep left at the next junction and drop down to the Anvil Inn and over the bridge across Kirkgunzeon Lane.

11. Turn right past the church to climb out of this pretty village. Ignore the turning to the left at the fork but at the T-junction go right for Drumcolton. Follow the lane onwards until it meets another at Killywhan. Turn right for Beeswing.

12. Join the main road again. Turn left and then right by the church to rise swiftly up to a watershed of Loch Arthur. The road then runs smoothly through the valley of the Glensome Burn to New Abbey. At the A710 turn right for the abbey, mill and village inn. Otherwise, go left towards Dumfries.

13. Turn next right for Kirkconnell, climbing up the hillside away from New Abbey and with magnificent views across to the ruins and Waterloo monument. Keep left at the sharp bend and follow this narrow lane to pass by Kirkconnell Tower. The road bends left and heads for the main road.

14. At the A710 go right and pass by the turn for Mabie Forest on the left. Cross the valley of Crooks Pow and climb to a cross roads. Go left here and ride along a tree-lined ridge lane. One mile on, turn right to run through the edge of a housing estate at Cargenbridge.

15. Meet the A711 road and turn right for the town centre. This joins the A780 road and continues ahead to the bridge over the Nith.

Cycling in Dumfries and Galloway (Dumfries and Galloway Tourist Board)

GREAT CYCLING IDEAS!

Cyclists are fond of tea-breaks and, according to health experts, both cycling and tea are good for you in moderation. The *Tetley Guide to Cycling in Scotland* (in association with the CTC) includes ten routes mainly in Strathclyde and Central regions. For a copy, contact Biss Lancaster plc, 69 Monmouth Street, London, WC2H 9DG. Tel: 0171 497 3001.

Another good idea to be found in Scotland are two breaks: Learn to Ride a Bike Week and Learn to Fix a Bike Week with Geoff Apps at The Schoolhouse, Milne Green, Coldstream, TD12 4HE. Tel: (01829) 382389.

Borders

Cycling in The Forest - The Tweed Valley: leaflet explaining off-road provision for cyclists in forests in the Tweed Valley.

Tweed Cycleway: ninety-mile route along the River Tweed between Berwick on Tweed and Biggar. A good base on which to build rides along the border. Leaflet available.

Central

Cycling in the Forest: cycling opportunities in Queen Elizabeth Forest Park. A Forest Map is also available. Price range: £1 - £2.

Glasgow to Killin Cycleway: a major route out of town into the Trossachs using the Loch Lomond cycle route and then north through Aberfoyle and Callander. Leaflet available.

West Highland Way: long-distance trail from Glasgow to Fort William through the Central Region. Hard going in places, very poor surfaces.

Dumfries & Galloway

Cycling in Dumfries and Galloway: a pack of four leaflets including Dumfries, Coast and Forest; Kirkcudbright and Coast; The Galloway Hills Grand Tour; Lockerbie. Another leaflet invites you to follow the KM Trail to the birthplace of the pedal cycle at a blacksmith's shop run by Kirkpatrick Macmillan, a genius whose invention changed the world of cycling. Tel: Dumfries and Galloway Tourist Board (01387) 50434.

Cycling in The Forest: a leaflet which describes over 200 miles in the forests of South West Scotland.

Northern Star Cycleway: a guide to 280 miles of adventure cycling from Middle England to the Scottish Border along the backbone of England. Contact: New Riders of the Open Road, address as below.

Scottish Border Cycle Way: a booklet describing a cycle adventure from Portpatrick, near Stranraer to Berwick on Tweed along the quiet roads of the Border country. Price: about £2.00 - £3.00. Contact New Riders of the Open Road, Laurieston Hall, Castle Douglas, Kirkendbrightshire DG7 2NB for details.

Fife

Fife Charter for Cyclists: a booklet which explains why Fife is gearing up to provide for the cyclist and what it is going to do about it. Priority is being given to a path between Dunfermline and Alloa.

Forests of Fife and Kinross: a leaflet describes cycle routes around Tentsmuir forest which is situated between the estuaries of the Rivers Tay and Eden.

Grampian

Discover Paradise: an 8-day tour (written up in a booklet) from Inverness to Stonehaven and Aberdeen. It is recommended that you plot the route on ordnance survey maps before setting off.

Highland

Cycling in The Forest, North Scotland: leaflet available. Small charge.

Great Glen Cycle Route: a route between Fort Augustus, Invermoriston and Loch Ness Youth Hostel. Leaflet available.

Speyside Cycling Initiative: known as Bike Spey-side, an Action Pack has been put together for cyclists listing possible off-road routes on the Glenlivet Estate and several road tours. Small charge. Tel: (01479) 810363.

Lothian

Cycle Routes in Edinburgh: a useful map and list of facilities for cyclists in Edinburgh. Ideal for both visitors and residents.

Cycle and Walk in Lothian: a leaflet describing cycling opportunities in Lothian. One of several leaflets suggesting places to cycle in Lothian.

Cycling in East Lothian: leaflet which highlights riding along the Haddington and Longniddry Cycleway (4.5 miles) and Pencaitland Railway Walk (6 miles) with a map which guides you along the minor roads on Edinburgh's eastern edge.

Cycling in West Lothian: leaflet available.

Innocent Railway: a route from Edinburgh to Musselburgh which follows one of the earliest railways in the UK from Edinburgh to Dalkeith. It was described as the Innocent Railway by Dr Robert Chalmers because it used horse drawn waggons which seemed so innocent in comparison to more sophisticated steam railways! Four miles of ride described in a leaflet.

Mountain Biking in the Pentland Hills: leaflet available.

North Edinburgh Cycle Routes: cycle tracks using the old Granton, Leith and Barnton branch railway lines. Leaflet available.

Strathclyde

Airdrie to Bathgate: a path being developed by Sustrans from Airdrie to Bathgate which eventually will link Glasgow to Edinburgh.

Glasgow to Loch Lomond Cycleway: a mainly off-road route to Balloch where you can picnic at Balloch Castle Country Park. The views across Loch Lomond are exquisite. It is a pity that cycling around the loch itself is not traffic free, but you can take a boat!

Glasgow to Irvine and Ardrossan and Kilmacolm: this includes a route out to Kilmacolm, Irvine and Ardrossan, mainly off-road, but using minor roads in places. Leaflet available. A Sustrans-built route as part of a network developed in Strathclyde with the support of local authorities.

Pedestrian and Cycle Routes in Strathclyde: a useful leaflet for those seeking routes in the region.

Tayside

The Green Circular: a leaflet explaining a cycle route in the Broughty Ferry and Monifieth area with a view to extending to a circular route around Dundee. Leaflet available.

The Islands

Most roads on the islands are ideal for cycling as traffic is limited and ferry companies accept bikes on board.

Cycle Holiday Companies

Achanalt House Guided Mountain Bike Holidays, Achanalt House, Achanalt by Garve, Highland IV3 2QD. Open: all year. Tel: (01997) 414283.

Ballantines, The Old Exchange, Hightae, Bridge of Dee Road, Castle Douglas, DG7 1TR. Open: all year. Tel: (01556) 4534.

Bespoke Highland Cycle Tours, The Bothy, Camusdarach, Arisaig, Highland PH39 4NT. Open: May to October. Tel: (01687) 5272. BR.

Bikebus, 4 Barclay Terrace, Edinburgh, EH10 4HP. A programme of days out, weekends and holidays between May and October using a bus to carry the bikes to a required location. This is not a packaged tour, however, and it is best to 'phone for details. Tel: 0131 229 6274.

Pinebank Chalets, Dalfaber Road, Aviemore, PH22 1PX. Open: All year. Tel: (01479) 810000.

Roundabout Scotland, 4 Observatory Lane, Glasgow, G12 9AH. Open: all year. Tel: 0141 337 3877.

Scottish Border Trails, Drummore, Venlaw High Road, Peebles EH45 8RL. Open: April to September. Tel: (01721) 722934. Off-road mountain bike trekking holidays.

Scottish Cycling Holidays, Ballintuim Post Office, Blairgowrie, Central PH10 7NJ. Open: all year. Tel: (01250) 886201. Well-established holiday company, also offering breaks in East Anglia too!

Strathspey Adventure, Ryvoan, Carrbridge, Inverness. Open: all year. Tel: (01479) 84667.

Trossachs Cycle Hire, Trossachs Holiday Park, Aberfoyle, FK8 3SA. Open:

Mid-March to October for holidays. Cycle hire all year. Tel: (01877) 382614. A great location for the Trossachs.

Wade Road Mountain Bikes, Slochd Cottages, Slochd, Carrbridge, Highland PH23 3AY. BR. Open: June to September. Tel: (01479) 841666. Specialises in mountain bike tours.

Wildcat Mountain Bike Tours, 15A Henderson St, Bridge of Allan, Sterling FK9 4HN. Tel: (01786) 832321. Tours available in May, September and October, but holidays can be arranged at other times at this independent hostel.

Cycle Hire Companies

Borders

Bowhill Estate: *Bowhill Trekking Centre*, Bowhill House, near Selkirk. Open: April to October. Tel: (01721) 722934.

Coldstream: *Neatwork*, PO Box 2, Guards Road, TD12 4NW. Open: March to October. Tel: (01890) 883456. Neatwork make and distribute very special bikes - hire for potential buyers only!

Craik : *Craik Trekking Centre*, west of Hawick. Open: April to October. Tel: (01721) 722934.

Glentress: *Glentress Mountain Bike Centre*, Glentress Forest near Peebles. Open: April to October. Tel: (01721) 722934.

Central

Stirling: *New Heights*, 26 Barnton Street, FK8 1NA. Open: April to October. Tel: (01786) 450809. BR.

Dumfries and Galloway

Castle Douglas: *Ace Cycles & Craigshiels Activities*, 11 Church Street, DG7 1EA. Open: all year. Tel: (01556) 504542.

Dumfries: *Grierson & Graham*, 10 Academy Street. BR. Open: all year.. Tel: (01387) 59483. They also organise a seasonal hire service at Mabie Forest; *Nithsdale Cycle Centre*, Rosefield Mills, DG2 7DA. Open: all year. Tel: (01387) 54870. BR.

Drumlanrig Castle: *Origamix*, The Craft Centre, Drumlanrig Castle, near Thornhill, DG3 4AG. Open: Easter to end September. Tel: (01848) 330325.

Gatehouse of Fleet: *KLR Cycles*, The Garage, Catherine Street, DGY 2JD. Open: all year. Tel: (01557) 814392.

Glenluce: *Belgrano*, 81 Main Street. Open: all year. Tel: (01581) 3554.

Kirkcudbright: *Gillespie Leisure*, Brighouse Bay Holiday Park, Borgue, DG6 4TS. Open: March-October. Tel: (01557) 870267.

Minnigaff: *Creebridge Caravan Park*, Minnigaff. Open: March-October. Tel: (01671) 2324.

Newton Stewart: *Merrick Caravan Park*, Bargrennan, DE8 6RN. Open: March to October. Tel: (01671) 840280.

Fife

Anstruther: *East Neuk Outdoors*, Cellardyke Park, Harbour Head, Cellardyke. Open: all year. Tel: (01333) 311929.

St Andrew's: *Gordon Christie Cycle Shop*, 86 Market Street, KY16 9PA. Open: April to August. Tel: (01334) 72122.

Grampian

Aberdeen: *Aberdeen Cycle Hire*, 188 King Street, AB2 3BH. BR. Open: all year. Tel: (01224) 644542; *Alpine Bikes*, 70 Holburn Street, AB1 6BX. BR. Open: all year. Tel: (01224) 211455; *Outdoor Gear*, 88 Fonthill Road, AB1 2UL. Open: all year. Tel: (01224) 573952. BR.

Braemar: *Braemar Mountain Sports*, Invercauld Road. Open: all year. Tel: (01339) 741242.

Buckie: *Horizon Cycle Hire*, 125 Main Street, AB56 1XT. Open: all year. Tel (01542) 833070. Accommodation available in summer.

Dufftown: *Mini Cheers*, 5 Fife Street, Dufftown, AB55 4AL. Open: all year. Tel: (01340) 820559.

Elgin: *Bike Speystyle*, 17 High Street, NV30 1EG. Open: All year. Tel: (01343) 543388.

Forres: *ReCycles*, Rafford, IV36 0RU. Open: all year. Tel: (01309) 672811.

Grantown-on-Spey: *Crann-Tara Guest House*, High Street, PH26 3EN. Open: Closed November. Tel: (01479) 872197. Accommodation available January to October; *Speyside Sports*, 47 High Street, PH26 3EG. Open: all year. Tel: (01479) 872946.

Huntly: *Nordic Ski Centre*, AB54 5NZ. Open: all year, weekends and holidays. Tel: (01466) 794428.

Keith: *Edintore Mountain Bike Hire*, Edintore Farm, AB55 3JP. Open: all year. Tel: (01542) 810245.

Kincraig: *Loch Insh Watersports*, Kincraig, PH21 1NU. Open: all year. Tel: (01540) 651272.

Newtonmore: *Craigower Lodge Outdoor Centre*, Golf Course Road, PH20 1AT. Open: all year, except mid-October. Tel: (01540) 673319. BR.

Peterhead: *Robertson Sports*, 1 Kirk Street, AB42 6RT. Open: May to September. Tel: (01779) 72584.

Tomintoul: *Bridge of Brown Tearooms*, Grantown Road, AB37 9HR. Open: all year. Tel: (01807) 580335; *The Gordon Hotel*, The Square, AB37 9ET. Open: all year. Tel: (01807) 580206. Accommodation available and holidays can be arranged.

Highland

Aviemore: *Ellis Brigham*, 9-10 Grampian Road, PH22 1RH. BR. Open: May to November. Tel: (01479) 810175; *Speyside Sport*, 64 Grampian Road, PH22 1PD. BR. Open: all year. Tel: (01479) 810656; *Sporthaus*, Sporthaus Building, Grampian Road. Open: all year. Tel: (01479) 810655.

Brora: *The Bicycle Bothy*, Ar Dachaidh, Badnellan, KW9 6NQ. Open: all year. Tel: (01408) 621658. Accommodation packages available. BR.

Cannich by Beauly: *Glen Affric Hotel*, Cannich, IV4 7LW. Open: all year. Tel: (01456) 415214.

Fort William: *Off Beat Bikes*, Macrae's Lane, PH33 6AB. Open: all year. Tel: (01397) 704008. Self-catering accommodation available. Plus *Great Glen Cycle Route* pick-up service; *Lees Cycle Hire*, Leesholme, Cameron Road, PH33 6LH. Open: April to October. Tel: (01397) 704204; *The Isles of Glencoe Hotel*, Ballachulish, PA39 4HL. Open: all year. Tel: (0185) 582 1582. Accommodation is available. BR; *Mountain Madness*, Albert Road, Ballachulish, PA39 4JR. Open: all year. Tel: (01855) 811728.

Inverdruie: *Inverdruie Mountain Bikes*, Rothiemurchas Visitor Centre, near Aviemore, PH22 1QH. Open: all year. Tel: (01479) 810787.

Inverness: *Pedalaway,* 7 Lovat Road, IV2 3NT. Open: May to September. Tel: (01463) 233456; *Thornton Cycles,* 23 Castle Street, IV2 3EP. Open: March-December. Tel: (01463) 235078. BR.

Kyle of Lochalsh: *Kyle Cycles,* Old Plock Road, IV40 8BL. Open: all year. except first half of October. Tel: (01599) 4842. Holidays can be arranged.

Lochcarron: *Bab's Bike Hire,* Sage Terrace, IV54 8QZ. Open: all year. Tel: (01520) 2370. Near to the famous Bealach-na-Ba.

Nethybridge: *Nethybridge Ski School,* PH25 3ED. Open: all year. Tel: (01479) 821333. Accommodation is available.

Spean Bridge: *The Great Glen School of Adventure,* PH34 4EA. Open: all year. Tel: (01809) 501381.

Strathpepper: *J.P. Cycle Hire,* Old Inn West, Blairninich. Open: May to September, but at other times phone first. Tel: (01997) 421710.

Torlundy: *Off Beat Bikes,* Nevis Range. See Fort William entry.

Lothian

Edinburgh: *Central Cycle Hire,* 13 Lochrin Place, Tollcross, EH3 9QX. Open: all year. Tel: 0131 228 6333; *Sandy Gilchrist Cycles,* 1 Cadzow Place, London Road, Abbeyhill, EH7 5SN. Open: all year. Tel: 0131 652 1760. BR.

Strathclyde

Arrochar: *Mr and Mrs Chandler, Lochside Guest House,* G83 7AA. Open: all year. Tel: (01301) 2467.

Barbreck: *Buidhe Lodge Mountain Bikes,* Craobh Haven, Barbreck. Open: all year. Tel: (01852) 5291 or 5677. Guided tours available.

Dunoon: *Tortoise Cycle Centre,* Highland Stores, 152-156 Argyll Street. Tel: (01369) 5959.

Lochgilphead: *Crinan Cycles,* The Pier Workshops, Ardrishaig by Lochgilphead, PA30 8DZ. Open: all year. Tel: (01546) 603511; *Mountain Bike Hire,* Barmolloch Farm, Kilmichael Glen, near Ford, PA31 8RJ. Open: all year. Tel: (01546) 81209. Cottage accommodation available.

Oban: *Oban Cycles,* 9 Craigard Road, PA35 5NP. Open: all year. Tel: (01631) 66996.

Motherwell: *Strathclyde Country Park, Watersports Centre,* 366 Hamilton Road, ML1 4ED. Open: March to November. Tel: (01698) 266155.

Glasgow: *Tortoise Cycle Centre,* 1417 Dumbarton Road, Scotstoun. Tel: 0141 958 1055; *Dales Cycles,*150 Dobbies Loan, G4 0JE. Open: all year. Tel: 0141 332 2705.

Tayside

Blair Atholl: *Atholl Activity Cycles,* Old School Park. Open: Easter to October. Tel: (01796) 473553. During the winter months cycles may be hired from Allt na Fearn, Killiecrankie, PH16 5LN.

Blairgowrie: *Ballintuim Caravan Park and Hotel,* Bridge of Cally, near Blairgowrie, PH10 7NH. Open: January to October. Tel: (01250) 886276. Holidays can be arranged all year; *Mountains and Glens,* Railway Road, Welton Industrial Estate, PH10 6EP. Open: all year. Tel: (01250) 874206. Trekking Holidays can be arranged.

Crieff: *R.S. Finnie, Crieff Cycle Centre,* Leadenflower Road, PH7 3JE. Open: all year. Tel: (01764) 652599. Holidays available from April to October; *Crieff Ski Shop,* 66 Commissioner Street. Open: all year. Tel: (01764) 654667.

Dundee: *Nicholson's Cycle Centre,* 2 Forfar Road, DD4 7AR. Open: (01382) 461212. BR.

Dunkeld: *Dunkeld Mountain Bikes,* The Chalets, Tay Terrace, PH8 0AQ. Open: April to October but November to March by prior arrangement. Tel: (01350) 728744. Guided tours and holiday available. BR.

Kenmore: *Perthshire Mountain Bikes,* Pier Road, PH15 2HS. Open: all year. Tel: (01887) 830291 (Summer) or (01887) 830414 (Winter).

Kinross: *Lochleven Cycle Tours,* Bowood, KY13 7LQ. Open: all year. Tel: (01577) 850213. Tours are available from June to September.

Pitlochry: *Pitlochry Mountain Bikes,* 18 Tomcroy Terrace, PH16 5JA. Open: February to December. Tel: (01796) 473298. Holidays are arranged from April to October. BR.

St Fillans: *Cycle Tracks*, Invernearn, PH6 2NF. Open: March to October. Tel: (01764) 685322. Holidays can be arranged.

The Islands

Arran, Brodick: *Brodick Cycles*, Opposite Village Hall, KA27 8DL. Open: Mid March to October. Tel: (01770) 302460; *Mini Golf Cycle Hire*, Shore Road, KA27 8AJ. Open: all year, but bookings preferred. Tel: (01770) 302272.

Corrie: *The Spinning Wheels*, The Trossachs, KA27 8JB. Open: all year. Tel: (01770) 810640. **Whiting Bay:** *Whiting Bay Hires*, The Jetty, KA27 8QL. Open: all year. Tel: (01770) 700382.

Cumbrae, Millport: *Bremner Stores*, 17 Cardiff Street, KA28 0AS. Open: Easter to October for cycle hire. Tel: (01475) 530309; *F&G Mapes & Son*, 3-5 Guildford Street, KA28 0AE. Open: all year. Tel: (01475) 530444.

Gigha: *J & M McSporran*, General Merchants, Ardminish, PA41 7AA. Open: April to October. Tel: (01583) 5251.

Lewis, Stornoway: *Alex Dan Cycle Centre*, 67 Kenneth Street, PA87 2DS. Open: all year. Tel: (01851) 704025.

Mull, Aros: *On Yer Bike*, Salen, PA72 6JG. Open: Easter to October. Tel: (01680) 300501.

Orkney, Stromness: *Orkney Cycle Centre*, 54 Dundas Street, KW16 3DA. Open: all year. Tel: (01856) 850255.

Skye, Ardvasar: *Skye Ferry Filling Station*, IV45 8RS. Open: March to October. Tel: (01471) 4249.

Broadford: *Fairwinds Cycle Hire*, Elgol Road, IV49 9AB. Open: all year. Tel: (01471) 822270. Accommodation available April to October.

Portree: *Island Cycles*, The Green, IV51 9BT. Open: March to December. Tel: (01478) 613121.

Uig: *North Skye Bicycle Hire*, Glen-Conon, IV51 9YA. Open: all year. Tel: (01470) 42311.

NORTHERN IRELAND

Includes the six counties of the province,
with opportunities also for cycling in Eire
Tourist Information: Northern Ireland Tourist Board,
59 North Street, Belfast, BT1 1ND. Tel: 01232 231221

Northern Ireland is as green as the guidebooks suggest. Being not much more than 80 miles in length and 110 miles wide, it is ideal for cycling. There are hill ranges such as the Sperrins in the North West, or the Antrim plateaux which bring a challenge to cycling here, but they are not as formidable as the Scottish Highlands. Several large natural lakes, known here as loughs, are also worth discovering. Lough Neagh is the most impressive, but Lough Erne is the prettier and Strangford Loch is probably the easiest to cycle around.

Some say the best cycling is in County Antrim, to the Giants Causeway, where impressive six-sided basalt columns can be seen. Ride down the coast and through the glens of Antrim to Ballymena and a different world is unfolded. Otherwise choose County Fermanagh to see the lakeland and possibly include a loop into the Clogher Valley.

There are also pleasant rides to the south of Belfast in the Mourne Mountains and down to the harbours of Annalong or Kilkeel.

The Ards Peninsula also offers an opportunity for cycling. This is where St. Patrick arrived in Ireland in 432 AD and there are reminders of this historic occasion throughout the 23 mile long finger of land. Ride through Greyabbey and along the shores of Strangford lough to its narrowest point at Portaferry where a ferry crosses to Strangford; both towns now are centres for fishing. A little farther south is Downpatrick where an impressive cathedral still stands on the ruins of several previous monastic buildings and churches. Down cathedral is where St Patrick is buried and this has been a scene of pilgrimage throughout the centuries.

Wherever you choose the certainty is that you will come across many ancient monuments which help to piece together the rich tapestry of life in Northern Ireland. You will also be assured of a welcome. There are no cycleways and very few facilities specifically for bikes because the traffic density on rural roads is so low thus making cycle touring in Northern Ireland a very enjoyable prospect.

COUNTRYSIDE RIDE

Fermanagh Lakeland

A lakeland tour with Mervyn Walker of Cycle-Ops, Kesh.

Distance: 52 miles.
Terrain: Easy Going.
Map: O.S. map sheet 17 Lower Lough Erne.
Cycle Hire: Cycle-ops bicycle hire at Kesh. Contact Mervyn Walker on (01365) 631850.
Accommodation and Refreshment: Available in the villages and towns along the route. Cycle-Ops can help with those wishing to camp. Telephone Tourist Information at Enniskillen (01365) 323110.

The Ride

Lough Erne in County Fermanagh, is beautiful cycling country. Lough Erne is divided into two by a narrow strip where the town of Enniskillen lies. The ride follows the rocky shores of Lower Lough Erne where there are dozens of small islands, which once were sanctuaries for early Christians, but have now returned to their natural habitats.

The ride also passes by many ancient settlements of the county, castles and garrison settlements built to defend this important route through Ireland. The fairy tale settings of the stone fortress towers standing in woodland and by sparkling waters belie the bloody power struggles of earlier centuries. There is so much to visit on the tour and it really is a picnic paradise, so allow two days.

Seeing Places

Belleek: on the lower reaches of the lough this settlement is famous for its pottery where intricate porcelain items are crafted with great skill. Belleek is also home to an annual fiddle festival, a celebration of traditional Irish folk music.

Enniskillen: is very much a crossing point of old highways between the

175

Upper and Lower Lough Erne with its straggling main thoroughfare running between the East and West Bridge. The remains of Enniskillen castle can be seen at the west end. There is a museum here reflecting local history. At the east end is a marvellous Victorian park on the lower slopes of Fort Hill.

Lower Lough Erne: offers a haunting aspect over numerous islands, chosen in earlier times as places of worship. It is possible to visit many of the islands on the route such as Devenish and Lusty Beg. It is also possible to join in several watersports at various points along the lough.

The Route

1. From the centre of Kesh follow the A47 in the direction of Belleek. After crossing the bridge turn left for Muckcross Quay. This brings you to the very edge of the lake and at the last car park follow the lakeside track for one mile to Drumrush caravan park. Turn right through the park and then left at the main road.

2. Cycle over the bridge onto Boa Island. Here a short diversion by boat can be made to Lusty Beg Island where there is a nature reserve and café. Otherwise continue along the A47 road to pass the carved figure of Janus in the graveyard of Caldragh, signposted from the main road.

3. Ride onto Castle Caldwell Forest where there is a nature reserve, a castle and the famous Fiddlers Stone at the entrance. There's also an ancient "cot" used until recently to carry cattle and other animals between the island on the lough.

4. Maintain your route on the A47 to Belleek where a stop off at the pottery is a must. On leaving the village take the A46 towards Enniskillen, enjoying great views on the climb to the Cliffs of Maho. Stop at the car park (Grid Reference: 062583) on the right and climb the steps to the top. The view across the entire length of the lough is exquisite. What better place for a picnic?

5. Continue along the A46 to Enniskillen, a section of the route which skirts the shores of the lough. Make a short detour to see the ruins of Tully Castle, a 16th century fortress, by turning left as signposted off the main road. On returning to the A46 turn left and ride into the county town of Enniskillen, a possible overnight stop.

6. Follow the A32 north for about 3 miles to Trory. At the garage turn left for the departure point for Devenish Island. Here the famous

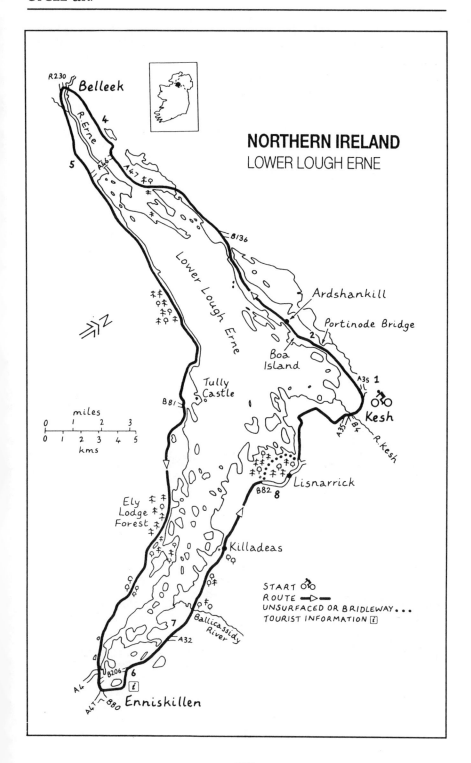

NORTHERN IRELAND
LOWER LOUGH ERNE

Belleek

R230
R.Erne
A46
A47
B136

Lower Lough Erne

Ardshankill

Portinode Bridge

Boa Island

2

A35 1

Kesh

A35
B4

R.Kesh

Tully Castle

B81

miles
0   1   2   3
0 1 2 3 4 5
kms

Lisnarrick

B82 8

Ely Lodge Forest

Killadeas

START
ROUTE
UNSURFACED OR BRIDLEWAY . . .
TOURIST INFORMATION [i]

7

Ballicassidy River

A32

B206 6

A4
A47 B80 Enniskillen

Round Tower can be seen. The monastery was founded in the 6th century. Return to Trory.

7. Take the B82 road for Kesh. Ride for 9 miles through woods and meadows to Castle Archdale country park, where there is a network of paths and tracks. There is also a marina where boats can be hired or you can take the ferry to White Island. From the marina, continue to ride through the wood to the old castle Archdale, the ruins of an ancient castle, dating from the early 1600s and not to be confused with the new Castle Archdale, which is late 18th century.

8. About one mile into the park where the road turns sharp left (at the end of a camp site) take the path to the right which leads into the forest. Approximately 100 metres up the track turn left and follow the forest path to the old castle ruins. On reaching the car park, go to the road; turn sharp left for the last hillier but inspiring scenic run to Kesh. There are several excellent views of the lough along here, glimpses of some of the loveliest waters to be seen in the UK. Return to the homely village of Kesh.

Cycling in Fermanagh (Northern Ireland)

GREAT CYCLING IDEAS!

Cycling Information Bulletin: there are few leaflets and booklets on cycling in Northern Ireland but this bulletin provides several suggestions for road cycling. Tel: Northern Ireland Tourist Board on (01232) 246609.

Cycle Holiday Companies

Ardclinis Activity Centre, 11 High Street, Cushendall, BT4 ONB. Open: all year. Tel: (01266) 771340.

Cycle-Ops, 31 Mantlin Road, Kesh, Co Fermanagh BT93 1TV. Open: all year. Tel: (01365) 631850.

Hilsea, 28 Quay Hill, Ballycastle, Co Antrim BT54. Open: March to November. Tel: (01265) 762385.

Lough Erne Cottages Ltd, c/o 9-15 Bridge Street, Enniskillen, BT74 7BW. Open: all year. Tel: (01365) 322608.

McCycle Tours, 2 Brookeborough Road, Maguires Bridge, Co. Fermanagh BT94 4LR. Open: All year. Tel: (01365) 721749.

Cycle Hire Companies

Belfast: *McConvey Cycles,* 467 Ormeau Road, BT7 2ED. Open: all year. Tel: (01232) 330322; also at 10 Pottingers Entry, BT1 2UP.

Castlewellan: *Ross Cycles,* 44 Clarkhill Road, BT39 9BL. Open: April to October. Tel: (01396) 778029.

Coleraine: *Car and Home Supplies Ltd,* 8-10 Queen Street, BT52 1BE. Open: all year. Tel: (01265) 42354.

Enniskillen: *Lakeland Canoe Centre,* Castle Island. Open: all year. Tel: (01365) 324250.

Lisburn: *John M Hanna Cycles,* 11-13 Chapel Hill, BT28 1EP. Open: all year. Tel: (01846) 679575.

Eire

If you are thinking of travelling to Eire, by far the best company to contact is *Irish Cycling Safaris,* 7 Dartry Park, Dublin 6. Tel: (00 353 1) 260 0749.

THE CHANNEL ISLANDS

These comprise six islands, the largest being Guernsey and Jersey

Tourist Information:
Guernsey (States of) Tourist Board, PO Box 23, White Rock, Guernsey. Tel: (01481) 726611
Jersey Tourism, Liberation Square, St Helier, Jersey. Tel (01534) 500 700

GUERNSEY

Guernsey is the largest of a group of islands which make up the States of Guernsey. There's now six circular waymarked rides on the island-details from TB. Of the associated islands Alderney, Herm, Lihou and Sark - it is the latter which can only be explored by cycle, horse-drawn carriage or on foot.

Cycle Hire Companies

St Martin's: *La Villette Garage Cycle Hire*, La Villette, GY4 6QD. Open: all year. Tel: (01481) 37577.

Vale: *West Coast Cycles*, Les Tamaris, Portinfer Coast Road. Open: all year. Tel: (01481) 53654.

St Peter Port: *Millard & Co Ltd*, Victoria Road, GY1 1HV. Open: all year. Tel: (01481) 720777; *Quay Cycle Hire*, White Rock. Tel: (01481) 714146.

Alderney: *Puffin Cycle Hire*, GY9 3XT Open: April-Oct, Tel: (01481) 823725.

JERSEY

Sunshine channel island with "Green Lanes" scheme welcomes cyclists, walkers and horses (not cars) across the island. There's more cycle hire now too!

180

Cycle Holiday Companies

Jersey Cycletours, 2 La Hougue Mauger, St Mary, Jersey JE3 3AF. Open: April to October. Tel: (01534) 482898.

Try also *Eurocycle*, Tel: (01534) 47775 or *Zebra* (listed below).

Cycle Hire Companies

St Helier: *C. I. Carriage Co*, 13 The Esplanade, Tel: (01534) 888700; *Lawrence de Gruchy*, 46 Don Street, Tel: (01534) 872002; *Doubleday Garage*, 19 Stopford Road, Tel: (01534) 31505; *Ezec Cycle Hire*, 22 Rouge Bouillon, Tel: (01534) 69287; *Good Health*, 79 New Street, Tel: (01534) 875057; *Hireride*, 1 St John's Road, Tel: (01534) 31995; *Rent-a-Bike*, 70 The Esplanade, Tel: (01534) 24777; *Zebra Cycles*, 9 Esplanade, St Helier, JE2 3QA. Tel: (01534) 36556.

Cycle hire also available at St Clements and St Lawrence.

Cycling in Jersey (Jersey Tourism)

ISLE OF MAN

An autonomous island with its own parliament (Tynwald)
Tourist Information: Isle of Man Department of Tourism,
Sea Terminal Building, Douglas. Tel: (01624) 686766

The Isle of Man is well-known for its annual Tourist Trophy (TT) motorcycle race, a noisy affair at the best of times (avoid the first two weeks of June). The island also hosts cycle races but, for the most part, the place is quiet out of the main summer season. The roads are wide and often quiet too. Cycling to Castletown and Port Erin, Ramsey and Peel or across the mountainous interior allows you to explore the Celtic and Viking heritage of the island.

It is surprising that the isalnd is not more popular for cycling as the roads are relatively quiet. A pleasant tour to Castletown by way of St Marks would bring the rider to the tidal harbour and the ancient fortress of Castle Rushen dating from medieval times. Until the middle of the last century it was the seat of government on the island. Continue to Port St Mary and Port Erin which have two of the finest beaches on the island. Return to Peel along the coast road. Peel Castle dates originally from the 10th century as does Peel church, both of which are situated on St Patrick's island overlooking the harbour. This is the centre of the island's kipper business and kippers are supplied throughout Britain from these curing houses.

There are also routes to the north of Douglas climbing to Snaefell summit and Ramsey. Return along the coastal route to Laxey with its impressive water wheel, 72.5ft across and said to be the largest in the world. This is a major centre for the electric tramway between Douglas and Ramsey as you can change for an exhilarating ride up to Snaefell (the easy way). The road through to Onchan Head is worth a detour for there are exceptional views across to Cumbria.

The Isle of Man welcomes cyclists and provides ample opportunity for a short break or holiday tour.

Cycle Hire Company

Douglas: *Eurocycles*, 8a Victoria Road, IM2 4EY. Tel: (01624) 624909; *Pedal Power*, 5 Willow Terrace. Tel: (01624) 662026.

Ramsey: *Ramsey Cycles*, Bowring Road. Tel: (01624) 814076. All open all year.

Above: The Wheel at Laxey, Isle of Man (Isle of Man Tourist Board)

Opposite: Cycling at Wetton Mill, Staffordshire Moorlands (Chris Rushton)

CYCLIST'S NOTEBOOK

Visitor Information

For Overseas Visitors:

Written inquiries:
British Tourist Authority, Thames Tower, Black's Road, Hammersmith, London, W6 9EL.

If in London, call at:
British Travel Centre, 12 Regent Street, Piccadilly Circus, London, SW1Y 4PQ.

TOURIST BOARDS

The addresses below are for written or 'phone enquiries:

Cumbria Tourist Board
Ashleigh, Holly Road, Windermere, Cumbria LA23 2AQ. Tel: (01539) 444444.

East Anglia Tourist Board
Topplesfield Hall, Hadleigh, Suffolk IP7 5DN. Tel: (01473) 822922.

East Midlands Tourist Board
Exchequergate, Lincoln, LN2 1PZ. Tel: (01522) 531521/3.

Guernsey (States of) Tourist Board
PO Box 23, White Rock, Guernsey. Tel: (01481) 726611.

Heart of England Tourist Board
Woodside, Larkhill Road, Worcester, WR5 2EF. Tel: (01905) 763436.

Isle of Man Dept of Tourism
Sea Terminal Building, Douglas. Tel: (01624) 686801.

Jersey Tourism
Liberation Square, St Helier, JE1 1BB. Tel: (01534) 500700.

London Tourist Board
26 Grosvenor Gardens, London, SW1W ODU. Tel: 0171 730 3450.

Northern Ireland Tourist Board
59 North Street, Belfast, BT1 1ND. Tel: (01232) 231221.

Northumbria Tourist Board
Aykley Heads, Durham, DH1 5UX. Tel: 0191 375 3000.

North West Tourist Board
Swan House, Swan Meadow Road, Wigan Pier, WN3 5BB. Tel: (01942) 821222.

Scottish Tourist Board
23 Ravelston Terrace, Edinburgh, EH4 3EU. Tel: 0131 332 2433.

South East England Tourist Board
The Old Brew House, Warwick Park, Tunbridge Wells, TN2 5TU. Tel: (01892) 540766.

Southern Tourist Board
40 Chamberlyne Road, Eastleigh, SO5 5JH. Tel: (01703) 620006.

Wales Tourist Board
Brunel House, 2 Fitzalan Road, Cardiff, CF2 1UY. Tel: (01222) 499909.

West Country Tourist Board
60 St David's Hill, Exeter, EX4 4SY. Tel: (01392) 76351.

Yorkshire and Humberside Tourist Board
312 Tadcaster Road, York, YO2 2HF. Tel: (01904) 707961.

Cycle Hire

USEFUL HINTS AND TIPS

❏ What deposit is required?

❏ Try the bicycle for size and comfort and adjust saddle accordingly, assuming the frame size is right.

❏ Is the bike equipped with a pump and puncture repair kit, (or puncture proof tyres), basic tools (adjustable spanner, spare inner tube, tyre levers) and an emergency contact number should things go really wrong? Most of the time they don't!

❏ Ask for the gears to be explained if you are not used to the type of bike provided

❏ Are there any route instructions or marked-up maps available?

❏ The very latest return time!

CYCLE HOLIDAY CHECKLIST

Before you book, ask yourself ten questions:

1. Is this a part of the country I wish to visit?

2. What sort of break do I want - an easy going short break, a gruelling mountain trip, or a softy option?

3. Are you interested in an independent tour or travelling with a group?

4. Is the company right? How do they respond to my request for information?

5. What exactly does the holiday include and exclude?

6. What accommodation is being used? Does it suit me/us?

7. What kit and back up is provided? Is it baggage transfer or is there a support van available if you become marooned somewhere?

8. What kit and clothing will I need?

9. How much extra am I likely to spend on the tour or independent holiday?
10. What insurance cover is there? What bonding does the company have should it find itself in financial difficulties?

(Adapted from a special report written by the author for *Bicycle 1993*).

Picture: Chris Rushton

Travelling by
Public Transport

TRAVELLING TO THE UK FROM ABROAD

By Plane: Most airlines carry your bicycle as part of the overall baggage, often wrapped in a strengthened cardboard box or special cover. Increasingly airlines are charging for the carriage rather than including it as baggage. Details should be obtainable at your travel agent at the time of booking. Those flying into Gatwick can seek cycle hire from Cycloan. Tel: (01293) 886598.

Through the Channel Tunnel: Provision is being made for the carriage of bicycles through the tunnel. Le Shuttle will carry cycles. There is a special coach and trailer for cyclists. Eurostar high speed trains (well high speed on the continent if not here) aim to allow bikes to be carried, probably 3 per train (of which 40 are planned) but details had not been agreed at the time of printing.

By Ferry: All of the ferry companies take accompanied cycles free or for a small sum (between £5 - £10 sterling at the time of writing).

TRAVELLING WITHIN THE UK

By Ferry: most ferries carry accompanied bicycles free of charge although there is sometimes a small charge on Scottish island routes and between Britain and Ireland.

By Train: the picture is confused at present, with the process of privatisation still in full swing. The new train operating companies seem to be taking cyclists more seriously. For example, North West Regional Railways Policy allows bicycles to be carried free of charge on most trains. On certain routes such as the Hope Valley line on Sundays and the North Wales Coastal service, cycles are being encouraged and on the latter some trains can still take tandems.

❑ InterCity usually allow no more than three bicycles per train and charges a reservation fee. The new Intercity companies are likely to maintain this or will possibly allow more bikes per train in some instances.

❑ Network South East allow bikes on most trains free and without a reservation. The obvious exceptions are commuter trains into and out of London at peak times.

❑ In general, the cross country runs which are operated by train companies, previously known as Regional Railways, allow one bike per train which must be reserved because, they say, of limited room on board. Look out for the latest leaflet from each company as they emerge. The situation is different in some of the major conurbations too. Merseytravel, for example, still allows bikes on trains without charge or reservation. They are welcome at all times except at busy rush hour. Merseytravel are progressive in encouraging sensible use of their rail services and the Mersey Ferries.

By Bus and Coach: Most bus and coach companies do not carry bikes on board. In rural areas on long distance routes, some drivers will put your bike in the luggage compartment.

There are a number of improvements for cyclists on the coach front including:

The Yorkshire Bikeliner: This service operates on a weekly basis from Hull, York, Leeds, Huddersfield, Manchester, and Chester to Dublin, Athlone, Galway and Limerick during the summer. It will also be useful for the Trans-Pennine route when open throughout. Tel: (01482) 882560 for details.

The European Bike Express: A specially designed coach service between Middlesbrough in the north-east and Dover/Calais. Contact European Bike Express, 31 Baker St, Middlesbrough. Tel: (01642) 240020/251440 for details.

Bicycle restrictions tend not to apply to folding bikes such as the Brompton or Bickerton, which fold up into a carry bag.

Cycling along Waterways

If you enjoy level cycling, industrial heritage in cities and lovely stretches through rural cuttings and across aqueducts then cycling along British Waterways' towing paths will be ideal. It is certainly traffic-free, but remember you share these paths with fishing folk, boaters and walkers.

The current position is that to cycle on any British waterways towing path you require a permit, for which there is a small fee. A recent review by British Waterways of the standard of towpath has meant that some sections will be open to cycling with care (Category A paths), others with extreme care (Category B paths) and some sections where cycling is not permitted at all on safety grounds (Category C paths).

There is no general public right of way for cyclists on British Waterways' towing paths, but cycling is likely to be allowed on A and B sections if you adhere to the following code:

THE WATERWAYS CODE FOR CYCLISTS

1. Access paths can be steep and slippery - join the towing path with care.
2. Always give way to other people on the towing path and warn them of your approach. A "hello" and "thank you" mean a lot. Be prepared to dismount if the path is busy with pedestrians or anglers.
3. You must dismount and push your cycle if the path narrows, or passes through a low bridge or alongside a lock.
4. Ride at a gentle pace, in single file and do not bunch.
5. Never race-you have water on one side of you.
6. Watch out when passing moored boats-they may be mooring spikes concealed on the path.
7. Take particular care on wet or uneven surfaces, and don't worsen them by skidding.
8. Never cycle along towing paths in the dark.

9. Towing paths are not generally suitable for organised cycling events, but your local Waterway Manager may give permission.

10. If you encounter a dangerous hazard, please notify the Waterway Manager.

Please remember you are responsible for your own and others' safety! You are only allowed to cycle the towing paths if you follow this code.

Before you cycle, contact the Local British Waterways Office. They are listed in local telephone books or 'phone Customer Services at British Waterways on (01923) 226422.

Picture: Chris Rushton

Cycling in Forests

The Forestry Commission has, in recent years, encouraged greater use of forestry through Forest Enterprise. This does not mean that all forests or all tracks within forests are open to cyclists. But an increasing number of routes are being introduced for use by cycle. These are subject, of course, to diversions when timber is being felled.

You will find that Forest Enterprise has waymarked many routes in several woods and, elsewhere, there are leaflets which explain where you should cycle. The potential for cycling off-road in woodlands is enormous and the newly-created urban forests around some of the UK's cities should hold even greater potential.

There is one cloud on the horizon. All of the good work being done by Forest Enterprise might well be undone by privately-owned forestry concerns should this government-backed body be dismantled and sold off. Pressure is mounting for this not to happen, but it is important that users seek access in newly-privatised woodlands as they are sold off.

The forestry routes through existing Forest Enterprise offer great potential for safe, off-road cycling as do the new urban forests.

Types of Bicycle

When buying a bike it is best to go to a well-established cycle trader who is knowledgeable about bikes and can provide after sales service - repairs, spare parts, etc.

It is also very important to buy a bike which suits your needs and fits you! Mountain bikes tend to be made in smaller frame sizes than touring bikes and a typical frame size would be 13 inches less than your inside leg measurement. With a touring bike it is likely to be 11 inches less. There's no better way than sitting on one in the shop or yard. Take your time as a bike is a major purchase.

There is also confusion sometimes about the types of bicycles manufactured to meet the needs of different segments of the UK market. The different types of bicycles are listed below.

Adult

Sports/Touring Bikes: designed for long rides; lighter and with five or more gears. They have full sized wheels and drop or straight handlebars. Panniers are used for carrying clothes and equipment.

Racing Bikes: specially-designed lightweight bikes built for speed. Ideal for racing competitions but of little value otherwise.

Conventional Adult Bikes: heavier-framed bikes with a limited number of gears, wider tyres and softer saddles. Designed for commuter activities and manoeuvrability in traffic. Usually with basket or panniers for carrying goods. They are sometimes referred to as "roadsters".

All Terrain Bike (ATB or Mountain Bike) & Hybrid: these bikes are built with a heavier frame, have an extensive range of gears (up to 21), wide tyres and are sturdily built for all terrains as the name suggests. The hybrid (sometimes referred to as 'trail and trekking' or 'town and trail' bikes) are roughly speaking a cross between the mountain bike and tourer.

Small Wheeled Bikes: these are designed primarily for short distance commuter or shopping trips, hence the name "shopper". They have small wheels and few gears. They usually incorporate a basket for carrying goods. A variation of these is folding bikes, which are attractive for those who use public transport regularly and need to carry their bike as luggage.

Tandems: these are bicycles made for two persons cycling together. In the early days of cycling, more optimistic machines were constructed:

The 1898 Ariel Pacing Quintuplet

Other Bikes

There is a range of other cycles such as unicycles and recumbents. They are specialised, but interest is increasing in the marketplace and manufacturers are always advertising in cycling magazines.

Children's Bikes

BMX/ATB style: heavier, small-wheeled cycles with wide tyres and low gear ratios. Styled to attract off-road riding or for stunt or circuit riding.

Other Children's Bikes: conventional cycles modelled on adult versions but with frame sizes suitable for children.

The 1818 Denis Johnson Hobby Horse (Mark Hall Cycle Museum)

Birmingham and Black Country Cycleway (Chris Rushton)

Cycling Facilities

Where you can cycle...

Highways

Cyclists can cycle on most highways *except* motorways or where prohibited locally, and this will be indicated by a sign (e.g., a pedestrian zone in a town). 'A' roads are, mainly, not places to cycle. 'B' roads vary enormously but, away from the main urban areas, they become far less trafficked and hence more cycle-friendly. 'C' roads (shown in yellow on Ordnance survey maps and not marked with numbers) and unclassified roads are the most appropriate for cycling, but conditions vary locally and according to sight lines.

Off-Road Routes

These routes are off the highway. They use mainly bridleways which are shared with walkers and horse riders. Thus, their surface is often very rough and they are suitable for mountain bikes only. Other routes use Byways Open to All Traffic (BOATS) which in reality have unmetalled surfaces and very low levels of traffic and Roads Used as Public Paths (RUPPS) which have a similar status to bridleways and thus are suitable for cyclists.

Two other main sources of off-road routes are forestry tracks in forests owned and managed by Forest Enterprise. These tracks are not metalled but are often waymarked and promoted specifically as routes for cyclists and sometimes horse riders. The other main off-road opportunities are canal towpaths shared with walkers, fishermen and boats mooring. These are currently controlled by means of a permit system which is under review (See 'Cycling Along Waterways').

Cycle Paths

The term 'path' is often used to describe a purpose-built cycle path along, for example, a disused railway. The facility will more than often be designed for use by walkers, cyclists and horse riders but often users are segregated. They are sometimes called railway paths.

Cycle Ways

Recommended, often signposted route in an area, usually linking attractions and accommodation and promoted as such. Such routes rarely deviate from the highway network but use mainly unclassified roads with low levels of traffic.

In urban areas, cycle lanes and tracks are used to a limited extent to provide safer routes for cyclists.

Cycling Organisations

British Cycling Federation: National Cycling Centre, 1 Stuart Street, Manchester, M11 4DQ. The recognised body administering track, road and off-road cycle racing.

Cyclists' Touring Club: 69 Meadrow, Godalming, Surrey GU7 3HS. Tel: (01438) 417217. This is the largest cycling association in the UK with approximately 40000 members with local groups throughout the country. It campaigns for improved facilities for cyclists, including those who enjoy cycle touring. For example, it is progressing one campaign *Help To Save Our Country Lanes* which is of direct benefit to all those who seek peaceful and safe access by bike into the countryside. The CTC offers a wide range of services for its members including:

▼ Touring holidays in the UK and abroad published in CTC Tours Guide

▼ Touring information and cycle routes

▼ Handbook packed with useful details and contacts

▼ Bi-monthly magazine 'Cycle Touring and Campaigning'

▼ Shop which sells cycling gear and publications

ETA: The Environmental Transport Association campaigns for a more balanced transport policy. It also offers a Cycle Rescue Package for members. Contact: ETA, The Old Post House, Heath Road, Weybridge KT13 8RS. Tel: (01932) 828882.

Friends Of The Earth: A long-standing campaigning group which has worked solidly for a sustainable environment. They have a transport campaign and cycling is a key area of interest. Contact: FOE, 26 Underwood Street, London. Tel: 0171 490 1555.

Green Flag International Ltd: This non-profit environmental organisation, dedicated to the development of a more sustainable travel and tourism industry, has established *Countryside Choice*. A new holiday information service for those wishing to visit the English countryside including cycling holidays. Either call (08910) 715700 with your holiday information request, or write to PO Box 396, Linton, Cambridge, CB1 6UL.

London Cycling Campaign: This organisation exists to represent the cyclist in Greater London. It lobbies for better facilities for cyclists including the implementation of a 1000-mile Strategic Network of cycle routes. Contact: LCC at 3 Stamford Street, London, SE1 9NT. Tel: 0171 928 7220.

Rough Stuff Fellowship: A well-established group for cyclists who love byways and tracks. Contact: Secretary, Belle Vue, Mamhilad, Pontypool, Gwent NP4 8QZ. Tel: (01873) 880384.

Sustrans: Sustrans is an abbreviation for "Sustainable Transport", emphasising forms of transport which do not pollute the planet for ever onwards and do not heavily consume finite resources. Sustrans is something of a cycling power-house which designs and builds traffic-free routes for cyclists, pedestrians and disabled people often in association with progressive local authorities. It is now developing the National Cycle Network, which will provide at least one safe, high quality cycle route within a ten minute bike ride of 20 million people. As a charity, Sustrans needs all the support it can muster. Contact: 35 King Street, Bristol, BS1 4DZ. Tel: (01272) 268893.

Transport 2000: A major transport campaigning group which advocates a major change in transport policy, including improved provision for bicycles. Contact: 10 Melton Street, London, NW1 2EJ. Tel: 0171 388 8386.

Routes in the Making

The breakthrough came on 11 September 1995 when the Millennium Commission approved a grant of £42.5 million to Sustrans to develop a National Cycle Network. The network is now being implemented and this will provide a boost for cycle tourism beyond our wildest dreams.

THE NATIONAL CYCLE NETWORK

Masterminded by Sustrans, the National Cycle Network will comprise 6500 miles of safe cycling. The aim of the network is to link town centre to town centre. This will enable people to cycle freely out of town into the countryside and vice versa, hence cutting down many of those unnecessary car journeys with the bike on the back of the car.

Approximately half of the network will be on traffic-free paths for shared use by cyclists and pedestrians. Half will be on back lanes or traffic-calmed sectors of towns. The core network, known as Millennium Routes will be available by the year 2000. This will include sections between Glasgow, Inverness and Aberdeen; Holyhead and Cardiff; Plymouth to Bristol and London. This will be followed by another five years of intensive building up to the Year 2005 linking in places such as Hull, Norwich and Weymouth.

The network is already beginning to take shape, but what is more important is that the concept has gained such wide acclaim that local authorities and other organisations are looking at schemes to progress in addition to the core routes. The potential for environmental improvement is enormous, especially in tourism, as this is a sector where there is great scope to introduce environmentally-friendly holidays.

THE PENNINE BRIDLEWAY

The bridleway is planned to run along the backbone of England in parallel with the walkers' route. It is designed for cyclists and horse riders as a 270-mile recreational tour from Hexham (rail station here) to

203

Wirksworth (railway station at nearby Whatstandwell). It should prove to be an excellent facility, but development has been dogged by those who resent cycle access into the countryside, although progress is now being made.

SKYE TO CADIZ

Sustrans and a consortium of local and regional authorities are investigating a route from the Isle of Skye to Cadiz in Spain under the European Union Atlantic Arc Alliance. It will make a superb cycle touring route. Buen Viaje!

THE TRANS-PENNINE TRAIL

This superb route across the Pennines from Liverpool to Kingston upon Hull (some 90 miles), linking with the Pennine Bridleway and passing through Woodhead, will mean that visitors from Denmark and Holland will be able to cycle directly from the arrival of their boat in Hull into the Peak District. Parts are complete now - see listings in the North West and South Yorkshire sections of this book - and the remainder should be in place by 1998 following a National Lottery boost in late 1995.

UK Youth Hostels

Youth Hostels provide inexpensive bunk-bedded accommodation in single sex or family rooms and dormitories. The hostels, often in historic buildings such as old water mills, mansions and schools, are clean and offer the basic comforts (and are graded according to facilities available). You have to join one of the Youth Hostel associations to enjoy the benefits of this wide range of accommodation.

ENGLAND AND WALES

There are 250 youth hostels in England and Wales. All welcome cyclists. The YHA also organises cycling and multi-activity holidays through its 'Great Escapes' programme so contact them for details: YHA (England and Wales), Trevelyan House, 8 St Stephens Hill, St Albans, Hertfordshire AL1 2DY. Tel: (01727) 855215.

SCOTLAND

There are over 80 youth hostels in Scotland offering comfortable shared accommodation. As in England and Wales, they are often in historic buildings of great character and in beautiful locations. All welcome cyclists and there are special packages available for cyclists. Contact: Scottish Youth Hostel Association, 7 Glebe Crescent, Stirling, FK8 2JA. Tel: (01786) 451181.

NORTHERN IRELAND

There are half a dozen well-situated youth hostels in Northern Ireland. Contact: YHA Northern Ireland, 56 Bradbury Place, Belfast, BT7 1RU. Tel: (01232) 324733.

You might also contact the Irish Youth Hostel Association (An Oige), 39 Mountjoy Square, Dublin. Tel: (003531) 363111 if you intend to travel to Eire where there are 44 youth hostels.

Further Reading

There is a range of magazines for the keen cyclist. Some target mountain bikers, others the racing enthusiast, but there are three which are more for touring cyclists:

Bike Culture: Available at specialist cycling outlets.

Cycling World: cycle-touring with an old-fashioned appeal.

Cycling Today and Mountain Biking: cycling issues, touring, off-road tips and technical know-how. A good all-round magazine.

Cycle Sport: as the title suggests!

Cycle Touring & Campaign: the CTC magazine which is packed with cycling matters but excels in its tours features.

London Cycling Campaign: the LCC has its own bulletin focusing on London issues.

Mountain Biker International: great magazine packed with ideas, kit checks, etc.

Mountain Biking UK: as above - ideal for mountain bikers.

Racing Cyclist: sport, sport and sport.

A useful booklet is "Cycle Away", a superb listing of all known cycle routes and initiatives updated periodically. Published by the CTC at approximately £2.

Sigma Press, publishers of this book, publish several other books covering the most popular cycling areas - see details at the back of this book.

The Off-road Cycling Code

1. Stay on the Trail
Only ride bridleways & byways - avoid footpaths
Plan your route in advance
Use the Pathfinder/Landranger Maps.

2. Give Way to Horses & Walkers
Make sure they hear you approach
Ride carefully when you pass.

3. Bunching is Harassing
Ride in twos or threes.

4. Be Kind to Birds, Animals & Plants
And keep your dog under control.

5. Prevent Erosion
Skids show poor skills.

6. Close Gates Behind You
Don't climb walls or force hedges.

7. Stay Mobile
Wear a helmet
Take a first aid kit
Carry enough food & drink
Pack waterproofs & warm drinks.

8. Take Pride in Your Bike
Maintain it before you leave
Take essential spares & tools.

9. Be Tidy
Take your litter home
Guard against fire.

10. Keep Smiling
Even when it hurts!

Source: THE OFF-ROAD CYCLING TRAIL GUIDE

WE WELCOME YOUR COMMENTS!

If you have any comments, suggested additions, corrections or updates you would like to make to **CYCLE UK!** please fill in the form below (please photocopy to avoid damaging the book):

Comment: ....

....

....

....

....

....

Name: ....

Address:...

....

....

Postcode: ....

Please send to Sigma Press, 1 South Oak Lane, Wilmslow, Cheshire SK9 6AR, or fax to 01625-536800. Tel: 01625-531035; E-mail: sigma.press@zetnet.co.uk

Tick here for a free catalogue ☐

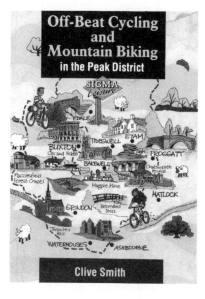

Also of Interest:

OFF-BEAT CYCLING IN THE PEAK DISTRICT – Clive Smith *(£6.95)*

MORE OFF-BEAT CYCLING IN THE PEAK DISTRICT – Clive Smith *(£6.95)*

CYCLING IN & AROUND MANCHESTER – Les Lumsdon *(£6.95)*

CYCLING IN THE LAKE DISTRICT – John Wood *(£7.95)*

BY-WAY BIKING IN THE CHILTERNS – Henry Tindell *(£6.95)*

CYCLING IN THE COTSWOLDS – Stephen Hill *(£6.95)*

50 BEST CYCLE RIDES IN CHESHIRE – Graham Beech *(£7.95)*

CYCLING IN OXFORDSHIRE – Susan Dunne *(£7.95)*

CYCLING IN SOUTH WALES – Rosemary Evans *(£7.95)*